Dwight Longenecker

THE GARGOYLE CODE

THE
GARGOYLE CODE

Dwight Longenecker

STAUFFER
BOOKS

STAUFFER BOOKS
Terra Lane, Greenville, SC

BOOK DESIGN & COVER ART
Christopher J. Pelicano

PRODUCTION COORDINATION
Richard Peck

PRINTED AND BOUND IN THE U.S.A
Color House Graphics

ISBN 978-1-935302-00-1

Contents

Contents

WEEK FOUR

WEEK FIVE

WEEK SIX

Contents

PASSION WEEK

EASTER

THE GARGOYLE CODE

A Letter to the Reader

From the Seventh Celestial Circle,

Greetings in the name of the Highest! All blessings to you from the Lord of Light and the Fire of Love. May you know the powerful purity of the most Blessed Lady, and the radiant goodness of all your brothers and sisters in glory. Alleluia! Amen!

Dear child, before you begin reading this book I wish to give you a word of warning. What you read here may disturb you. The smoke and stench of hell itself reeks in these pages, and it was much debated among us whether it should be released to you at all.

However, the times are so perilous and the battle so intense, that it was decided in the courts above that it is better for you to look over the shoulders of the dark ones than to fall into the trap of forgetting their existence.

The servants of the Dark Lord love to hide. They flourish in the shadows and thrive when you do not believe in them. They love nothing more than for you to be complacent and negligent and lazy. Remember dear one, that the fiends are like beasts stalking their prey. Camouflage and subterfuge are their tools. They are masters of deception and they serve the Lord of the Flies, the Father of Lies.

In reading the correspondence we have chosen to release, you will find yourself entwined in a web of deception and counter deception. You may feel soiled by the enemy's vulgarity and sickened by his coarse speech. You may become depressed and despondent at the complexity of the enemy's plan. You may become confused by his strategies and bewildered by his cunning chicanery.

When this happens, look to the light. One moment of honest prayer and adoration will open the windows of your soul. Look upward to the clear, fresh breeze of the North. Instantly you will be given the child like simplicity which your soul requires. At once you will see what you should do. Then ask for the grace to run from the darkness into the light and this grace will be given. Laugh at his pride and self deception, laugh and be free for he has already been defeated.

We have released the correspondence of the fiends during the time when they know the battle is greatest. This blessed time of Lent is when we take the battle to them. Dear child, if you could only see what great things are accomplished in the spiritual realm by your earnest prayer, your sincere fasting and your self sacrificial giving to the poor! The fiends hate these disciplines with all their heart, and remember, they hate you too. They want to utterly destroy you. They would devour you if they could.

You will have heard of other letters that have come from the depths of darkness. The letters of the fiend Screwtape were released many years ago. Do not be surprised if these letters are similar to those that have gone before. Remember, the dark ones cannot create anything new. The only power they have is to twist and distort what the Great and Only Father has created. The poor wretches have only a few tunes to sing and a few tricks to play. Their existence is in a continuously downward spiral, and the only hope they have is to try to drag human souls into their vortex of destruction. Once you see their sad lack of creativity you will realize that these letters could only be repetitive and monotonous.

So read these letters day by day in these blessed weeks to prepare your soul for the great Paschal Feast. Read them as part of your warfare with the dark ones. Read them for the purification of your soul. Read them as an act of intercession for others you know of who are lost in the dark. Read them and act on them in prayer. We have not released them for your entertainment, but for your enlightenment.

And now I must urge you to something which may not be pleasant for you. Please know that I make this request out of great and radiant love for your soul. I must urge you with all the power and grace within me to read this correspondence as you would read a mirror. As the fiends discuss the poor souls in their charge, see yourself. Do not read in a detached manner as if you are reading about someone else, but engage your heart. Ask for the light to see how you are like the poor souls in these pages. Only then will you be able to spot the fiend's activity in your own life.

If you are able to do this the benefits will be great. Go on this journey with joy. Remember, I will be there--full of light--to aid you on the journey. The Great and Good Lady of All Graces will blaze into your heart the Light from her Son who is the Lord of All Light, and the great peace that is beyond all earthly knowing will fill you. The graces of the Risen One will surround you, and you will be re-made into his likeness, who was first made in your likeness, so that when the day comes you will rise with him on his joyous Eastertide.

Peace be with You,

Your Guardian

THIS YEAR
Decoded Transmissions

Last February the listening posts of the International Intelligence Agency intercepted and unscrambled a series of messages that were sent electronically from sources unknown to destinations that have yet to be specified.

These communications were filtered out from the millions of faxes, text messages, emails, internet forums and telephonic electronic impulses radiating through the atmosphere. They were disguised and coded within the billions of electronic mail signals transmitted and received everyday, but seem to originate from a communications system that is independent of yet parasitical on, the normal global electronic communication systems. Computer programs have now been able to unscramble and decode the messages.

Experts are still unclear who composed or sent the messages, but they seem to be instructions and training for undercover agents working in the field of religious propaganda. The first of the messages is incomplete. The fragment reads...

...As the most recent communiqué has made clear, the new technologies of communication are to be exploited for our own ends. Now that our clients have developed such ingenious means of communicating with one another invisibly, it might occur to some of them that other invisible means of communication, like extra sensory perception, intuition, and even spirit channeling are possible. This interest may be developed into a passion, then an obsession until the individual invites you to either appear visibly or occupy his physical form.

This is a classic tactic. Down through the ages we have been very successful in using human fascination with their own technology to lure them into the dark labyrinths of the occult. How fondly I remember the wizards, magi and sorcerers. They started with books and experiments, and ended with spells to turn lead into gold and create potions that guaranteed eternal youth. They are not really not so different from the computer boffins, genetic engineers and plastic surgeons of today who begin by being enchanted by their own technology and end up being enchanted by one of us.

You will naturally want to encourage this, because you think that from such interests you will be able to lead the gullible brutes into the delightful playground of spiritualism, theosophy and the occult proper. This may be effective for some of the humans, but I would advise you not to overestimate their gullibility. Unhappily, most of them are rather level headed and regard spiritualism and the paranormal as a silly past time for foolish old women.

Their present disbelief in anything supernatural provides the best working conditions for us. They may not believe in miracles and life after death, but that also means they don't believe in us, and they certainly don't believe in the possibility that we might infest their bodies. This is just what we want. Enemy agents are always most effective when no one believes they exist.

Although it is attractive and sometimes pays dividends, encouraging the hairless chimps to explore spiritualism and the occult is more often counterproductive. If they go down that route they may actually start to believe in the supernatural, and before long they may start to take the claims of our enemies seriously.

Instead of the obvious route of tempting them into the occult, simply get them obsessed with the cleverness of their new playthings. In time you may get the females in your ward to use the internet for high speed gossip and endless shopping. Use the technology to lure young men into an addiction to pornography or role play games. With a little bit of finesse Dogwart, you will be able to lead the women into vanity and pure spitefulness while they indulge their greed while convincing themselves they have got a bargain. Meanwhile you may lead the men into a fantasy world of sloth and lust and that is only one step away from the warmth of our eternal home.

Finally, be on your guard. This week begins the season the enemy call Lent. Despite our success in turning this into a time for 'sharing with others', some of the enemy's agents still take prayer and fasting seriously. Watch out for them. The self righteous little cretins make me want to vomit up all the exquisite bile I have been imbibing. Step on them Dogwart. Crush the vermin...

At this point the transmission is interrupted.

A few days later another fragment of the mysterious messages was intercepted, de-coded and translated...

WEEK ONE ~ *Shrove Tuesday*

Dear Dogwart,

So you have seen the excesses of Mardi Gras in New Orleans and got all excited have you? How amateurish of you to start frothing at the mouth with anticipation! How little you know your own patient! I have checked the files on him Dogwart. A lily livered Catholic boy in his mid twenties is not going to suddenly descend into serious decadence. Having gone to that Catholic High School, the enemy's agents have unfortunately honed his moral sense. As a result he's likely to feel guilty just thinking about a girl in a bikini, and your hopes of him getting 'down and dirty' as you so crudely put it, are nothing but ridiculous fantasy. You don't seem to realize that little brats like him are actually repulsed by the more extreme forms of fun. The flamboyant decadence enjoyed in San Francisco and New Orleans is a bit rich for the little greenhorn. It's an acquired taste dear boy! Too much too soon and they run away. You need to lead them downward slowly but surely.

Ignore Fat Tuesday, Mardi Gras, Shrove Tuesday—whatever you want to call it. You may get him to take a few risks at a party or overindulge in some way, but the most predictable result of your bringing Fat Tuesday to his attention is that he will most certainly remember that tomorrow is Ash Wednesday, and what we don't want him to do is attend Mass and go through that ridiculous ceremony where they smear ashes on their foreheads.

Block the whole thing out of his head Dogwart. Remind him of a television program he likes, then get him to sit there all night and watch whatever banal trash comes on the screen. Make sure he has a big bag of snacks and a half gallon of ice cream. Once he's sated he might sit there for hours simply hopping from one channel to another. Get him into this state of mind, and keep him there, and he'll be yours forever. Make sure he does this alone. Before long he'll be in a downward spiral of loneliness and depression, and then you can really have some fun.

In my younger days I had several patients who might have accomplished great things for the enemy, but I succeeded in getting them to fritter away literally years of their lives watching mindless drivel on television. In the end their brains were fried very nicely and they not only stopped having creative thoughts, they stopped thinking altogether. Both of them grew enormously obese, missed the chance of marriage and one of them eventually descended into depression and blew his brains out. Messy for the cleaning lady, but satisfying; very satisfying indeed.

I know this sort of tempting is boring at first Dogwart, but persistence yields great rewards. Babylon wasn't built in a day! We must learn to accept some drudgery as part of the price of our freedom. I realize that these souls are utterly boring, and when they finally make it onto our menu they are as bland as tapioca pudding. Never mind; we must all earn our bread and butter dear boy.

Slubgrip

WEEK ONE ~ *Ash Wednesday*

Dogwart,

You really don't know what "all the ashes fol-di-rol' is about"? You should have mastered this in your basic training. Don't underestimate the enemy Dogwart. What you perceive as silly mummery and play acting they take very seriously.

They smear ashes on their heads today as a sign of 'repentance'. 'Repentance' is their term for groveling before the enemy and pretending to be sorry. The ashes are supposed to remind them that they are from dust and ashes and will return to dust and ashes. They actually seem to enjoy saying 'sorry.' It's the same disgusting enjoyment they get in having a hot bath; they all but grunt in their piggy pleasure. I hate it Dogwart! It turns my stomach to see them line up with their solemn faces and bowed heads! Then they play their funereal music and go home feeling all holy. Ashes! They want ashes! I'll show the nauseating chimpanzees ashes—but not before they have some flames first! Lord Below Dogwart! I'd love to get some of them down there where they belong! I'd love to practice my old pitchfork skills and turn a few of them on the slow rotisserie. That'd show the hairless bipeds.

What is most maddening is that you and I know what sort of stuff they're up to. That fat man, who has lied and cheated his way to the top, parades down to get his ashes like an innocent child. That skinny woman who thinks she's beautiful? We know about the affairs when she was young. We know about the abortions, the betrayals and the manipulation of men with her sex appeal. Then she minces forward in her little high heels and plays the penitent! It's all fake Dogwart, believe me. It's all make believe. None of them really mean it. They only do it to show off and make themselves feel better.

Even worse is the fact that the enemy encourages their pathetic little play. He's shameless! He actually seems to like it when they grovel and apologize all the time. And then he blames our Father below for being proud! The hypocrisy of it turns my stomach!

By the way, you can learn to mind your own business if you please. I know my patient attended Mass this morning. Don't worry. I've got my man firmly in control. You don't seem to realize that they can go to Mass and go through all the routines and miss the point entirely. I've got my patient wrapped up in ultra conservative Catholicism. Yes, he went to Mass and received his ashes, but all he thought about was the fact that the visiting priest's homily was too informal and folksy, and that he came out of the sanctuary to share the kiss of peace with the congregation, and that this was a liturgical infraction.

It was by the very fact of attending Mass and keeping the rules that I was able to keep him in a nice state of spiritual pride. Trust me dear boy, it takes some finesse to get a patient to live constantly in a state of spiritual pride, but the achievement is very pleasing. The delightful thing about spiritual pride is that the patient really does believe himself to be good, and he is therefore invulnerable to anything the enemy's agents throw at him.

You'll do well to avoid criticizing your betters Dogwart. Leave my patient to me and pay attention to your own. You're so pleased that your boy didn't go to Ash Wednesday Mass, but where did he go? My agents in charge of the internet tell me that he went on to a Catholic website, suddenly remembered that he hadn't been to Ash Wednesday

Mass and before bed made what they call 'an act of perfect contrition.' You lose Dogwart. That was far more of a real blow than my man actually going to church.

Slubgrip

WEEK ONE ~ *Thursday*

Dear Dogwart,

You will have noticed that the Catholics like to 'give something up' for Lent, and you will naturally think this should be discouraged. You're wrong again. Let them give up something for Lent. Let them give up chocolate or cookies or even booze. There's not much harm in it as long as you keep their minds focused on what they're giving up, and ensure they forget that they are also supposed to pray and give alms to the poor.

Get them all involved in the 'giving up game' Dogwart. Get them to talk endlessly about what they are giving up. With a little bit of ingenuity you will be able to plant a nice little seed of spiritual pride. If you can't do that, make sure that all their talk of 'giving something up' is as deep as their observance of Lent becomes. Glibtiggle once had a female patient who was so obsessed with giving up cream and sugar in her coffee that she thought of nothing else for the whole forty days.

My advice is to leave them with their pathetic attempt at asceticism. Of course you will find it hard to resist the odd poke. If you get bored I admit its fun to tempt them with the thing they have vowed to give up. Resist the urge. More often it is counterproductive. Remember Dogwart, while they are disgustingly physical, you should not mistake their repulsive physicality with stupidity.

Should you tempt the patient who has given up chocolate with chocolate fudge cake with hot fudge topping he will probably spot it straight away and sidestep. If he gives in and eats the chocolate cake you will feel pleased with yourself. Don't. Your patient (if he is even the tiniest bit serious about fasting) will instantly realize he has broken his vow, and repent. Any repentance is to be regretted enormously, but your amateurish attempts will actually be counter productive because not only will your patient repent, he will turn back to his fasting with renewed determination.

Try instead to focus his mind on the actual process of fasting. Remind him all the time that he actually is fasting, and how difficult it is. With luck he will focus so much on fasting that he will forget to pray. If possible get him to tell others about his fast. Get him to compare his austerities with theirs (and for badness sake, don't allow him to compare with someone who actually fasts more rigorously than he does or you might spark off the beginnings of humility in your patient). As you keep his mind on his fasting, remind him how good it is to concentrate on what he's doing. With some patience you will soon be able to develop the beginnings of some nice self righteousness, and with skill over time you may be able to develop your patient into a full blown Pharisaical prig. There is no harm in him fasting twice a week on bread and water if you can get him to be proud of it. Ah, the crunchy texture and bittersweet taste of really good self righteousness! They never make a main course, but they do make a very fine dessert.

I must go Dogwart. My patient has developed some pains in his side. Learn from everything dear boy. My tactic will be to make him worried about the pain. I can use this during Lent to get him thinking about himself. Its pathetic how a little bit of pain can turn these miserable half breeds into helpless animals.

Our work is thankless Dogwart.

Slubgrip

WEEK ONE ~ *Friday*

Dogwart,

Don't try my patience today Dogwart. You know Friday is a bad day for me. It gives me a headache dear boy. My poor sinuses! It feels like my head is actually being crushed.

You are bragging that your patient has dropped out of college, and that you have edged him into it as a result of a failed love affair and poor grades as a business major. This is indeed a step forward, but do you have a long term plan? He may drop out of college, but then what? I'll bet you hadn't thought of the next step at all. It's typical of you younger generation—always looking for the fast return and the instant pay off.

So your patient is feeling depressed and lonely? He is feeling like a failure and a misfit? So he is feeling unloved and unwanted; a loner and a loser? This is nothing Dogwart. Every one of them feels that way in their twenties. Just when they have everything going for them they feel most sorry for themselves. You think it is your own doing. It's not. Its simply one of their silly phases of 'growing up.' The skill is not in getting a patient in his twenties into this state, but what you actually do with it in the long term.

Jump on it Dogwart! Kick the sniveling little runt while he's down. Tell him he really is a failure and a loser, and that he will always be a zero. You won't get him to top himself, but you may be able to lay down a good foundation of self-hatred that you can build on gradually. Get him involved in introspection and self analysis. This is a good time to introduce him to the sort of 'counseling' that will encourage him to blame everyone else for his problems and see himself as a victim. Get him to blame his parents, make him see how they have messed him up. With any luck you will get him to hate his mother and father, and do so with a nice touch of self-righteousness. A good counselor will get him mouthing something like, "Of course I really pity my parents. They are victims too; in their own way." You'll soon get him to hate his parents, while never imagining that he is breaking the enemy's fourth commandment.

However, don't overestimate this dark mood of his Dogwart. At this age they're fickle. Tomorrow the sun may come out and a girl may smile at him and he'll feel invincible once again. Especially don't underestimate the enemy. What you have yet to learn is how quickly the enemy's agents can turn every little success of ours into their own triumph. As soon as the little brutes are down and out they sweep in like shameless scrap merchants to pick up the wrecks and rehabilitate them.

Stanksizzle once lost a patient at just this stage: the case history is in all the old textbooks. The patient (named Francesco) was in his twenties— a depressed, lonely coward; a spoiled middle class brat who became a soldier for the glory of it, then ran away from battle. Stanksizzle had him about to throw himself out of a high window, and before you could say "Hells Bells" the enemy had given him some sort of 'illumination', and the next thing you know the boy has rejected his perfectly acceptable merchant father, stripped off his clothes and left home to live as a pauper, rebuild a little tumbledown church, feed lepers and 'listen to God.'

This would have been a perfect opportunity to get an inside view of the enemy's more insidious forms of attack, but at the point of the enemy's 'illumination' Stanksizzle claims he couldn't hear what was going on and that he was blinded by the light. (Despite having his hindquarters gnawed on for the last 800 years, the coward is still complaining and blaming others for his monumental failure)

This is what can happen Dogwart. Be warned. Out of the depression and despair you have so carefully cultivated, the enemy will suddenly give them a way out. If you're not careful the enemy may turn your boy's failed love affair into a vow of celibacy and make him realize that he never wanted to be an accountant anyway and join the Franciscans.

Be like a lion Dogwart, stalk your prey. It's good to be hungry, and remember the motto of our Father below, "Eat or be eaten."

Yr mentor,

Slubgrip

WEEK ONE ~ *Saturday*

Dear Dogwart,

You will remember from your days of basic training how to keep your patient from that odious occupation called prayer. The astonishing thing is that the little chimpanzees actually believe they are talking to the enemy himself, but we know the enemy doesn't care a button about the little worms. How could he when he is obviously so superior to them? Still they want someone to talk to, so they talk to him, and when they do, it somehow transforms them. It is all play acting dear boy, but it needs to be discouraged nonetheless. We don't want them thinking that they are on the enemy's side, and we certainly don't want them behaving that way.

Happily, in this matter we rarely have to go beyond our basic training. You know the ground rules: keep the brutes busy and distracted. It is better to keep them busy and distracted with all the delightful entertainments of our world, but if that fails, keep them busy with what they think is the enemy's work. I had one female patient who spent her entire life running around 'helping people'. She thought she was doing 'the Lord's work' when in fact I had very carefully made her into the most troublesome gossip and busybody. In the end she was obsessed with her mission to help others, and when she was brushed off or didn't receive the gratitude she wanted she was deliciously horrible to everyone. I still remember with a thrill the tone of her voice when she would whine, "All I've done for you and this is the thanks I get!" Even when the silly cow came down to us she was looking for people to help. The 'others' down below soon gave her the truth about herself. She was eaten up by it.

I'm happy to say that keeping the little rodents busy and distracted works for most of them most of the time. However, should your patient decide to take prayer seriously (and during this season they call 'Lent' that is a real possibility) make sure that he spends all his time asking the Enemy for things he wants. The pleasing thing about this is that the thickheaded little amateur doesn't even know what he wants, and so he will very likely ask for things which, if he got them, would only help to bring him closer to our eternal feast. Your patient may try to experiment with other forms of 'prayer' like liturgical prayer, adoration, meditation or contemplation. If he does, make him feel bored, restless and irritated. Remind him how many important things he has to do, and that he is really wasting his time. He'll soon get up off his knees.

Most of all, keep your patient from the most horrible practice of praying the Rosary. How I hate the clattering of those tacky beads and the sound of old ladies (of both genders and all ages) rattling off those silly repetitive prayers. It stinks Dogwart! It's so common--so lacking in taste!!

Do you know when it comes to 'praying my beads', even some of my most educated and sophisticated patients don't seem to mind behaving like fat, Italian peasant women? I've seen a perfectly respectable college professor--a man who otherwise was one of my most successful cases--suddenly start reciting the rosary. He even bought beads that smelled of roses and kept them in a plastic box with a picture of that nauseating little French girl Therese Martin. It's unimaginable that the Enemy would stoop so low. It's a cheap trick, Dogwart; a schoolboy's practical joke. It's cheap, nasty and just plain disgusting.

I must go. I've just noticed that my conservative Catholic patient has started to read a book by a Catholic charismatic called *The Holy Spirit Heals Today*. This could be very dangerous!

Yours in haste,

Slubgrip

WEEK TWO ~ *Sunday*

Dogwart,

I see that your patient has gone to church. Take your tail from between your legs my dear fellow, it's not as bad as it seems. The first thing to be grateful for is that he has chosen St Cuthbert's—a church which is as shallow as he is. He's a sentimental sort of fellow who assumes that the feel good liturgy and 'folk' music we've been so successful in getting into most Catholic parishes is all there is on offer. Of course, he's never really had the opportunity to experience truly beautiful and awesome Catholic worship. Happily the music of the enemy's finest composers lies moldering in church cupboards nibbled by mice and consumed by damp, and most liturgists are obsessed with making the 'worship experience relevant.'

As a result he simply goes along with what is on offer. When he comes into church he switches off, tolerates the middle aged women warbling to flower power tunes and just puts in his time. Let him coast along Dogwart. The banal music, the trite politically correct sermons and the folksy style seem completely harmless to him, and that's what we want. We want him to feel that Mass is a warm, non threatening experience. Lull him into a sense of well being dear boy. As long as the Mass is a form of liturgical muzak it really will become the opiate of the people.

What we don't want is for him to start questioning things. He's in a miserable state, but he mustn't imagine that his faith might actually work or that it might offer him the way out of his present predicament. Keep the two parts of his experience totally separate. On the one hand, continue to keep him in the dark swamp of confusion, fear and loneliness. On the other hand, keep him going to a church that is so anodyne and watered down that he'll never once imagine that it could do anything other than put one to sleep.

In fact, Dogwart, this sort of church is rather like euthanasia—it's a form of spiritual mercy killing. Through it we've been able to gently lull millions of Catholics into a long, quiet spiritual torpor until they finally end up in our mansions below—having drifted there with a soporific grin on their foolish faces.

Your boy's priest is a tremendous help in this respect. Long ago he abandoned any idea that the faith has a supernatural dimension. He picked up the idea that he should be a social worker in a clerical collar about the same time he picked up the woman he maintains as a 'companion.' I heard him mouthing one of my own arguments not long ago to a priest friend: He said, "Celibacy simply means that I have promised not to get married. It doesn't mean I have promised not to have a relationship with a woman." We've managed to ensure that this priest is an awfully nice fellow. Everyone loves him for being so warm, so engaging and such a "good preacher". (By 'good preacher' they mean he tells lots of funny stories in his sermons) No one would dream of asking questions about his lady friend or the expensive vacations they take together.

So don't feel too bad about your patient going to that church. Keep him there; in fact I encourage you to make sure he remembers to go to Mass there every week. As long as he does he'll be quite safe.

Slubgrip

WEEK TWO ~ *Monday*

My Dear Dogwart,

For your own education I must add a short note to let you know how things have turned out with my conservative Catholic patient. In my earlier days I would have been alarmed at the sight of him picking up a book with the title *The Holy Spirit Heals Today.* I have no doubt he picked it up because of the twinges he has been experiencing in his right side. Such books can be very dangerous. With all sorts of sneaky euphemisms like 'healing' or 'the deliverance ministry' the weasely authors actually discuss (and I hate to even whisper the word) 'exorcism.'

Such things do not alarm me now. Instead of distracting my patient or telling him such a book was dangerous, I encouraged him to read it.

Now Dogwart, this is the delight of a particular finesse that comes with a tempter of my skill and experience! I not only encouraged him to read the book, but I reminded him that a Catholic of his maturity, spiritual insight and knowledge was duty bound to read such a book, and to do so with all his critical faculties in place. I reminded him of the verse from their own 'Scriptures' that he had a responsibility to 'test all things' to see whether they were of the Spirit.

It wasn't long before he had written off the whole book as a load of sentimental, heterodox and dangerous nonsense. It doesn't matter that the book was actually written by an adept and thoroughly 'orthodox' theologian, and was not nonsense at all. What matters is that my patient perceived it as such. You see, for a very long time now I have been constructing a nearly watertight, intricate and interlocking set of assumptions and prejudices in this particular patient.

I have encouraged his reading of spiritual books and his enthusiasm for all the outward signs of his religion. I have encouraged his tendency to pay attention to detail and his inclination to criticize those who are different from himself. This has led him to an exquisitely constant attitude of being critical and suspicious toward any aspect of religion that was unlike his own. By making sure that he believed he was right in all things and had nothing to learn I was soon able to guarantee that he would, indeed, learn nothing.

It worked like magic Dogwart! The patient took our point of view without the least bit of effort from me. All my hard work has paid off! I'm sure you will excuse my glee, but it really is enjoyable to see yourself doing something well. It is a justifiable delight to get things right, to know you've done it right and to realize that there really is no one quite like yourself in all the universe. One day Dogwart, you may ascend to such heights.

I think there may be something wrong with my patient. He is increasingly restless, and has discussed with his wife whether he ought to make an appointment to see his parish priest. This may be something to be concerned about, and I will keep you posted so you can learn how to handle such cases.

I wish you well,

Slubgrip

WEEK TWO ~ *Tuesday*

Dogwart,

It was sweet of you to congratulate me on wrapping things up neatly with my conservative Catholic patient, but is it possible that you can be quite so obvious and ignorant? First of all, you should know that your shameless flattery will not blind me to your underlying laziness and sneaky manner. Then you toss off the inane comment that you are glad that conservative Catholics are a 'spent force.'

You don't get it do you? The conservative Catholics are anything but a spent force. Some of the enemy's best warriors are conservative Catholics. Unlike many who call themselves Christians, they understand that they are engaged in a spiritual battle, and that there is all eternity to play for. They actually believe in us Dogwart! They are among the few who do anymore, and those who believe in us are far harder to tempt than those who imagine that we are no more than the stuff of medieval fairy tales or a projection of the collective unconscious.

You don't seem to understand that my success with my patient had nothing at all to do with the fact that he was either conservative or Catholic. The same temptation into self righteousness and a judgmental attitude work just as neatly for Evangelicals and Liberals. Some time ago I had a charismatic Christian pastor on my books. He was one of these 'Bible only' fellows, and unfortunately he started to read some books on Catholic apologetics. His 'Bible only' creed started to falter when he started to understand that there would be no Bible if it weren't for the authority of the Catholic Church that established the Bible in the first place.

To make matters worse he met one of the worst sorts of Catholic Christians: a layman who actually understood his faith and could defend it. Before I knew it, the Charismatic pastor was starting to take the claims of Catholicism seriously.

The same ploy I used for my conservative Catholic patient worked for the Charismatic pastor. I encouraged him to explore the Catholic faith further. I reminded him that he needed to be fair and read both sides of the question. I brought him across one of those anti-Catholic books that pretends to be scholarly, but is full of half truths, misconceptions and downright fibs. I told the Charismatic pastor to 'test all things'. (I also reminded him that his wife would have a fit if she knew he was thinking about Catholicism, and that he would lose his friends, his livelihood and his career as a pastor) He soon dropped his Catholic friend and he is now the head of his own denomination and still delights in 'testing all things' for himself.

The same applies to the so-called Liberals, except for the fact that with them you don't need to tempt them at all. They take it as one of their basic assumptions that you can't take anyone's word for anything, and that they have to exercise their 'critical judgment'. As a result they pick apart every belief and moral principle until there is nothing left. The most delightful thing about the liberals is not only that they do our work for us, but while they pride themselves on being critical of every belief, assumption and dogma, they are never critical of their own. They never stop to question whether being critical of everything is actually the way to discover truth or not. Consequently, we have them in the most pleasing double bind, in which they believe themselves to be open minded and enquiring, when in fact, they are the most bigoted and close minded humans of all.

So we encourage them to 'test things'. Of course we don't want them to truly 'test all things'. There's nothing worse than one of the vermin developing a truly open mind and an honest curiosity. When this is combined with the courage to go wherever the 'truth' (whatever that is) takes them, the results are truly dreadful to see.

No, you want to make them think they are 'testing all things' while you are quietly making sure your patient only reads the books we want him to read. You must get them into a situation where they are their own spiritual masters. Make sure they are certain what is right for themselves spiritually. Don't let them take anyone else's word for it. This is the surest way to make sure they learn nothing new about the enemy, and do virtually nothing of real value for his side of the fight.

The delightful thing is, by getting them into this state, they will imagine that they are actually very good Christians, and that since they know all there is to know they are moving gloriously upward to the enemy's home. I cannot express how pleasing it is Dogwart, when these self righteous souls come into our realm and suddenly realize with total surprise and dismay that their eternal home is not pie in the sky, but grit in the pit.

I admit, this tactic calls for real skill. Getting them to 'test all things' involves some risk. The danger sign is when your patient says (and really means it) "I don't know." At that point real curiosity may begin, and he might actually learn something new. Dogwart, believe me, at that point the enemy's agents are very quick off the mark. They move at incredible speed to enlighten the wretched little chimps with new understandings and insights. Keep your patient out of that state of mind. Get him to truly believe that he has an open and inquiring mind, while at the same time keeping him proud of what he knows, and confident that he has all the answers. That's the way to keep him on the broad path.

Chin up Dogwart, and don't be afraid of taking some risks. I look forward to your next report.

Yrs,

Slubgrip

WEEK TWO ~ *Wednesday*

My dear Dogwart,

I suppose you must be granted some modicum of praise for getting your patient to spend two hours last night looking at pornography on the internet, but I don't think you need be quite so triumphant. Garble said she spotted you and Squirmtuggle sniggering like schoolboys over the event. Don't get too big for your britches. You have probably overplayed your hand just for your own cheap thrills.

The problem is dear boy, that such tempting is simply too easy, and the results are often very slim. It is true that the new technology allows easier access to pornography, and we have more men addicted to smut than ever before. It is also true that multitudes are sliding down to our eternal home by wallowing in the juicy sins of the flesh, but what you don't seem to realize is that these men were already well on the way to the cauldrons before they became addicted. Most of them never had their consciences formed by the examples and teachings of the enemy.

If they did, they lost all sense of there being such a thing as sexual sin by the promiscuous society we have worked so hard to cultivate for the last one hundred years. They are sliding down the trash chutes into our incinerators not even knowing what they are doing.

Your patient is not one of these. You seem to forget that he has been formed in the ways of the enemy. He believes in all the enemy's sentimental myths of sin and forgiveness and redemption and all that blather. When you tempt him with the sins of the flesh your measly triumphs are very likely to be counterproductive. Did you get him to look at internet pornography? Did you get him to pleasure himself? Oooh, what a clever tempter you are! But while you were giggling about it with Squirmtuggle, and boasting to your friends; you probably never noticed that your patient was thoroughly ashamed of himself, and was already turning as fast as possible back to the enemy. The next thing you know he will be going all the way and lining up to make his confession. Then where will you be? It will have been one step forward; three steps back.

If you are to succeed in this area dear boy, it is going to take some hard work preparing the ground. You must undermine his whole worldview, and this takes time and effort. He has to change what he thinks about himself, the world and everything, or all your tempting will be wasted. Before you can get your patient seriously addicted to pornography and the sins of the flesh you have to get him to understand that the so-called 'sins of the flesh' do not matter. There are two ways to do this, both of which seem contradictory, but which have the same pleasing result.

The first way to achieve this goal is through the 'healthy' approach. Get your patient to read a good 'self help' book by one of our better psychologists. He will learn there that 'repression' of the sexual drive is downright unnatural and unhealthy. He'll learn that 'sexual expression' is normal for a young man, and that there is nothing more ordinary and natural than a good old fashioned tumble with a wholesome young woman. He needs to see that sexual relationships are like tennis—good fun if you have an able partner. He should cheerfully conclude that the whole sex thing is no more or less important than any other sport or past time. If you can get him to see that a 'variety of sexual expression' is important, he'll soon look tolerantly on things that he used to think were perversions, and before long he'll be thinking that it might be fun to give them a try.

Of course, while you are showing him that sex is as fun and as wholesome as a Coca Cola advertisement, you must be careful to hide from him the fact that this 'healthy' past-time is where he is most likely to pick up an incurable sexually transmitted disease. You must also make sure he doesn't read too much psychology or he will come across some other studies showing that if he is sexually promiscuous he is more likely to become depressed, dependent on drugs and alcohol and incapable of committing himself to a permanent relationship. The main thing at this point is to get him to change his mind about sexual activity. If he can see that it is just healthy and 'no big deal' you will then be able to lead him on very nicely to where we want him.

The second way to make him believe that sins of the flesh do not matter is the 'spiritual' way. This way is more subtle, but it can be very effective. Our first successes along these lines were with a delightful group called the Gnostics. You must look them up sometime in the *Infernal Encyclopedia*. With this tactic we accelerate the patient's spiritual life. Load him up with spiritual reading and spiritual experiences. Then help him to see that all that really matters is the 'spiritual', and that what is 'spiritual' has nothing to do with the flesh. I know it sounds ridiculous, but they really do fall for this one more easily than you might think. You know you've got your man when he indulges in pornography or some sin of the flesh, and then turns immediately to Bible reading and meditation without seeing any contradiction.

Get him to partition the behavior we want from his 'spiritual' behavior. Keep them in separate compartments in his mind. He will soon really believe that the dark and delightful things we are providing for him have nothing to do with his spiritual life. Dogwart, I am not exaggerating, we have had Catholic priests who were addicted to child pornography, monks who were abusing children and a bishop who actually raped a girl, and they went about their 'spiritual' lives as if nothing were the matter.

When they were caught, their simpering little 'flocks' were totally surprised and shocked. They thought these fellows really were 'great preachers' and 'wonderful pastors' and 'loving priests' but they were cut off from their own dark side because their tempters had drawn them very neatly into this trap.

So, do you see dear boy how it is all far more complicated than your sordid little triumph with your patient? If success is to mean anything at all, I'm afraid it will require far more diligence, intelligence and subtlety...traits, I must say, that do not come naturally to you.

While we are on the subject, I have asked Pipteazle to write to you about the sexual temptation of females. It's good to know how the other half live.

Yr mentor,

Slubgrip

WEEK TWO ~ *Thursday*

Ms. Pipteazle
Archsecretary Female Division
Lilith Hall, Seventh Circle

Dogwart,

Slubgrip has 'asked' me to write to you about the temptation of females. Lord below! As if I haven't got enough to do without wasting my time trying to school pipsqueaks like you in stuff you should have mastered in basic training. If you had read my manual *Vanity and Vixens* (which Knobby still has in the syllabus) I wouldn't have to take time now to bring you up to speed. However, when Slubgrip 'asks' it is foolish to refuse.

It's simple squirt. There's no point trying to tempt females with pornography. The female of the species simply isn't interested. They're far too practical to care about pictures of naked people. When they see the stuff they are either disgusted, somewhat curious (I say, that's a very athletic position to be in!) or they are just amused and dismissive. They've got their own peculiar weaknesses, and it has to do not with their eyes, but with their imaginations.

The female equivalent of pornography is romance literature, soap operas, and women's magazines. Some of our best writers work in this area. The reason women are not attracted to pictures of sexual activity is because they are more interested in the relationship than the sex. If we can get the female to see relationships from our point of view, then we have won. The best way to do this is for them to imagine the sort of relationships we want. Once they have dreamed of romance, they will try to find it in real life. Soap operas, romance literature and women's magazines are our most important tools.

You see, the females identify with the heroines of the romance stories. All we have to do is make sure the heroine behaves the way we want and the females will soon follow. The ideal modern heroine is a working girl. She is glamorous, beautiful, wealthy and intelligent, and she 'makes her own choices' about sexual partners. Our romantic heroine is a girl with high values and standards. She will only marry the perfect man, but until he comes along she sleeps with every good looking man who comes into her life. The men are never quite the perfect prince charming. In fact, they usually let our heroine down very badly, but she bounces back and before long she's in the sack with another fellow and life is beautiful again. Our heroine is a female knight errant—she's on a wonderful and exciting quest to find love. Try to watch one of our best television shows on this: it's called *Sex in the City*.

Do you see how brilliant this is Dogwart? The females are far more likely to swallow this stuff, never dreaming that there is anything wrong with it. Unlike your squalid pornography (which often even disgusts the men who look at it) no one dreams that romance novels and women's magazines are harmful in the least. Furthermore, most men are unlikely to act on the sexual fantasies you tempt them with. With the females the opposite is true. They are very likely to swallow the romantic dream hook line and sinker and fall for the first cad who comes along with a sweet pick up line. They'll go home with him, go the whole way and wake up the next morning. He'll think she was a common slut, but she imagines that she is a glamorous, honest and courageous modern woman who 'makes her own choices' sexually.

The whole game is far superior to your crude escapades you little runt. Not only do we have a whole generation of women locked into the lifestyle we want, but they believe they are wonderful people for doing so.

A final word: don't overlook women's magazines and gossip columns. I try to get girls as young as twelve and thirteen to start reading these. They're quite a brilliant invention. Our best gals down below have done a super job. The best of these publications are bright and colorful. They are filled with pictures of happy, good looking teenagers, and the pages are full of harmless chit chat about boys and school, and 'what color flip flops are people wearing to the beach this summer?" Then we pop in an article about sex which assumes that all healthy teenagers are already engaged in full sexual activity. The article might be a cheerful discussion of contraception, abortion or sexually transmitted diseases, and the 'write to us for advice' page will be full of letters from girls who are asking specific questions on advanced sexual matters.

I'm happy to say that this sort of literature is freely available to women and young girls and most of the vapid bipeds don't even blink twice at it. I have one patient who subscribes to this magazine for her twelve year old daughter because she thinks it helps the girl to 'cope with the real world.'

Our teen and women's magazines and all our literature is now a tidal wave of delightful material, and most of the little skirts have never imagined that it might be harmful. I know Slubgrip thinks it is common and cheap, but what do I care? It works. It keeps the 'down escalator' crowded, and as you and I know, our Father below does not judge on style, but results. Speaking of results, Dogwart, there are whisperings that Slubgrip is not too pleased with you at the moment.

Watch your back little fellow. Slubgrip has been around a long time. I wouldn't be surprised if he has plans to have you for dinner, if you catch my meaning.

More tomorrow,

Pipteazle

WEEK TWO ~ *Friday*

Ms. Pipteazle
Archsecretary Female Division
Lilith Hall, Seventh Circle

Dogwart,

I know you probably enjoyed my letter yesterday, but you're going to have to make do with just one more note from me about the female bipeds. I'm busy on my new training manual, *The Futile Female*. It's a summary of all our work over the last hundred years promoting something called 'feminism'.

A little runt like you will never understand the huge amount of work we have put in on this. The fact that the males you are tempting are by and large pusillanimous wimps is partially due to the work we have been doing with the females. One of the greatest strokes of genius in our work was to call the movement 'feminism' when there is nothing feminine about it. Nothing gratifies me more than to see some of our most pleasing female humans squawking about 'feminism' while sporting tattoos, butch haircuts, wearing overalls, and clodhopper boots.

Squeeztartle can tell you about the political successes we've had with feminism, but I need to outline for you how we use feminism to tempt the females sexually. It is really quite brilliant, Dogwart. If you want to master the art of deception and double talk you must attend some of my master classes here at Lilith Hall.

The first step of indoctrination is to show the females that they have been repressed and abused by men throughout human history. They have been forced to stay at home 'barefoot and pregnant in the kitchen.' We never allow them to see that for most women throughout history staying at home in the kitchen was the soft option. While they stayed home, their men were out doing back breaking work and risking their lives in the factories, the mines, the farms and the fields of battle.

They must see that the invention of artificial contraception is what liberated the females. We show them that it gave them 'reproductive freedom'. It is a short hop from there to get them to see that they have 'sexual choices'. From this point we neatly insert the illusion that the modern female can choose whoever she wants to have sex with whenever she wants it. If the silly blonde doesn't actually 'want sex' very often, we have a wide range of messengers from movie stars, pop singers and magazine editors who will convince her that something is wrong, and that if she isn't a virtual nymphomaniac she is unhealthy and abnormal.

Our most successful cases will therefore have sexual relations with any man who shows even the smallest amount of interest in her. She'll behave as, what her great grandmother would have called, a 'common slut' all the time being proud of her 'sexual freedom'.

Now here's where the really brilliant bit comes in Doggy. I love this so much I can hardly stop grinning at the thought. We are aware that if we get the females to behave this way they will actually be disgusted with themselves, and be unhappy. You see, unlike the males, they don't really want endless, meaningless sexual encounters. They want what the enemy wants them to want: a permanent, meaningful relationship. So when they become unhappy, instead of blaming themselves for their loose behavior, we get them to blame the male. Part of feminist theory is that the bad guys are the guys. We get them to believe that men, just by being men, oppress women. We've even been able to integrate some neat slogans like, 'All men are rapists'.

There is a whole genre of self help literature out there for the females which bemoans the fact that men are 'afraid of commitment' and when they walk out on the girl they are abandoning her and abusing her in a different way. It never occurs to the little vixens that the man might walk out on her because she is a slut, and he's looking for something better.

Do you see how it works Dogwart? We get the little fools to have sex with every man who comes along, while at the same time getting them to hate every man who comes along. As a result countless of the silly cows end up getting old, losing their looks and having nothing left but their 'careers'. Then it is an almost indescribable pleasure to get them to wake up one morning and admit to themselves that what they thought was a 'career' was really just a life of hard work and drudgery (usually for a man who is their boss), and what they really wanted all along was a loving husband, a large family, a house with a big kitchen full of children, a dog, three cats and the time to bake cookies. Then, when they realize it is too late to have any of those things their despair is most delicious.

I hope you have taken all this in runt. I don't want to have to waste more time with you in the future.

Pipteazle

WEEK TWO ~ *Saturday*

Dogwart,

I know I advised you to get your patient to attend St Cuthbert's parish, but what on earth are you doing allowing him to fall in with that young parochial vicar? You were supposed to allow him to trot along to a sleepy little Mass from time to time and lull him into spiritual complacency.

Now my sources tell me that he has actually gone out for a drink with the parochial vicar and that crowd of nauseating groupies that he surrounds himself with. I've never seen such a disgusting swarm of sycophantic losers. "Oh Faaather! this..." and "Faaather, that." It makes me sick. The fact that the young priest actually doesn't take himself very seriously, knows how to drink and tell a decent joke is even more irritating. That he wears his cassock everywhere and really does seem to take the Catholic faith seriously is not only annoying. It's dangerous.

And you didn't see it coming? Honestly, dear boy, what do I have to do? Spell it out for you? Then you try to blame me for advising you to send him to that church, and you say I should have warned you! Dogwart, you had better watch your step. I don't think you realize just who you're talking to. Despite my problems, you know I have achieved the thirty second degree of master tempter of the seventh circle, and you presume to blame me for incompetence?! Tempters have gone to the barbecue pit for less.

All of this comes to my attention on a Friday, when you know I suffer from the most terrible migraines. Never mind. I will try to overlook it dear boy. Just don't let it happen again. You really must keep your patient away from that priest, and his nauseating coterie.

By the way, what are your patient's eating habits like? He's not doing anything sneaky like fasting is he? One of the enemy's greatest tricks is to get our patients to fast secretly. They quietly skip lunch or avoid alcohol on a particular day, and the negligent tempter can miss what is happening for weeks. It is one of the disadvantages of our not having bodies. We forget how important physical things are for the miserable half breeds.

It is difficult for you to understand Dogwart, but because they are half animal and half spirit, what they do with their bodies affects their souls. This is why gluttony and sloth and sexual indulgence and drunkenness really matter. These things aren't really that harmful in themselves (unless of course you can lead them into addiction). Instead the over indulgence clouds their spiritual capacity. It makes them drowsy and induces a nice physical torpor which incapacitates them. It dulls their senses, and the sense it dulls the most is their capability to pray and do the enemy's work, and eventually it puts them on a path away from the enemy and toward our home below.

On the other hand, when they practice sexual continence, drink in moderation and fast, all sorts of terrible things happen. First of all, they become more adept at self control and discipline. This is never a good thing. Once they take control of their appetites Dogwart, it is only a short time before they take control of themselves, and then before you know it they will be taking control of you.

Secondly, fasting helps them control all their other instincts. They soon find that they have more control over their temper, their lust and their loose thoughts. The worst effect of fasting is that they become more alert and focused. Their senses are keener, and this means their spiritual senses are keener too. The patient who fasts is more aware of us, more aware that there is a battle going on, more aware of the enemy's agents working in his life, and more aware of the enemy's insidious and constant presence.

I'm going to be checking up on that patient of yours Dogwart. I suspect the little cretin is a sneaky fellow. He's showing too much interest in religion right now, and I wouldn't put it past him to be doing some sort of secret penance of fasting that is getting past you without you even being aware of it. If this turns out to be true, I'm beginning to suspect that you are on the wrong assignment. Your patient may simply be too much for you to handle.

Be vigilant Dogwart. The eye is everywhere.

Yr mentor,

Slubgrip

WEEK THREE ~ *Sunday*

Dear Dogwart,

Are you worried that it is Sunday and your patient might remember to go to Mass? I'm sure you've remembered the basic plays from the playbook for the weekend:

Make sure the patient starts the weekend in the right way. Get him out and about on Friday night. Keep him out as late as possible, and when he gets home encourage him to stay up until the wee hours watching anything that is on television. Tell him there is nothing wrong with this. He is "just relaxing."

Make sure he oversleeps on Saturday morning. Keep him in bed as long as possible. This will throw his sleep cycle out, and he'll be sluggish all day. If he stays in bed long enough, you've got him into sloth, which may lead to some other self indulgent actions. With a bit of skill you can get him to spend the whole day wallowing in laziness and self indulgence of one sort or another.

Encourage him to stay up late on Saturday night. Get a friend to invite him to go out to something he can't resist. Make him forget to set his alarm clock. He'll never be able to get up on Sunday morning for Mass, and when he misses he won't blame himself because, "He just forgot to set the alarm clock."

I know how mundane and dull this sort of tempting is Dogwart, but it really is our bread and butter. I realize the big flashy theft, adultery and violence that leads to disgrace and utter ruin is more fun, but it's the little successes that build up bit by bit to really bring a soul down to our Father's home.

Have you checked to see if your patient buys into this silly notion that to miss Mass is a "mortal sin"? (Such a quaint term don't you think?) The Catholic priests used to peddle this one quite heavily. It was in their interests to do so. Their gullible flock would certainly not sacrifice an hour of their time to sit in a dark, drafty church early on a Sunday just to endure dreary hymns, a dull sermon about sin and a sloppy liturgy with bored altar boys picking their noses.

I have to hand it to them, it is a clever marketing ploy: "Come to Mass every Sunday or risk burning in hell forever." Very neat and effective, and it worked for a long time. The little lemmings trooped off to Mass as they were told, but they neglected everything else about the enemy, so we still got a huge number of them in the end anyway.

I'm sorry to admit, however, that this rule also brought an unhappy number into the enemy's territory forever. It burns Dogwart, it burns with a terrible inner fire to see one of your patients start going to Mass because he fears hell, only to gradually start attending out of a sense of duty. After that it was terrible to see how many of them actually started to understand the Mass, and before long they had started to actually enjoy the nauseating habit of worship and prayer. This is what is so very insufferable about the enemy. He really doesn't seem to mind taking the little vermin for the wrong reasons. He says he wants them to "love Him freely" (whatever that nonsensical phrase means!) but he still accepts them if they come only looking for a fire escape from hell. It's despicable Dogwart. It's mean and cheap and vulgar. The enemy has no taste. That's his main problem.

Happily, the idea that missing Mass is a mortal sin is now pretty far from the imagination of most Catholics. We have the priests themselves to thank for this. For the last forty years they have been so frightened of making any of their flock feel guilty, that they have carefully avoided speaking about any sin at all, much less trying to promote the preposterous idea that their people might risk hell because they missed Mass. The delightful thing about all this dear boy, is that the same priests are now wringing their hands and wondering why Mass numbers are dropping, and there are no vocations to the priesthood and the religious life.

For forty years they have been telling their people that it doesn't matter if they miss Mass, and that they can be just as holy if they are married lay people with fat bank accounts as if they were celibate priests or nuns under a vow of poverty. Then they are surprised when the people say, "Alright then father, I guess I'll opt for being a married lay person then, and if it doesn't really matter if I go to Mass, I guess I'll hit the golf course instead." What has surprised me Dogwart, is how easily the Catholic priests fell into this trap. All we did was make them feel guilty about making people feel guilty, and everything else fell together like a collapsing cup.

The problem is, these Catholic teachings are like weeds. They keep coming back. I'll bet that odious young parochial vicar believes it's a mortal sin to miss Mass. You watch him Dogwart. He's a charming rascal. He won't preach it in the old fashioned way. He'll slip it into a conversation naturally. Someone will ask him when they're having a drink and he'll smile sweetly and say, "But of course it's a mortal sin to miss Mass. It you miss Mass you have decided not to receive God, and to reject God is a mortal sin."

I hate it Dogwart! I can't bear it when they use that kind of subterfuge; disguising what is a subtle and complex theory in language that appears straightforward and sensible.

Step on him Dogwart. Trample the nauseating little rodent. Find out his secret sins, and let Stanksizzle know. By Lucifer, we'll pull him down.

Get to work boy,

Slubgrip

WEEK THREE ~ *Monday*

Dogwart,

Do you remember my patient was reading a disturbing book called *The Holy Spirit Heals Today?* I have to tell you a most amusing story. My patient was reading this book because the twinges of pain in his side were getting more severe.

He was frightened enough to actually consider checking out a local parish where the priest has what he calls a 'healing Mass'. In the end he decided to make an appointment with his parish priest. This is undoubtedly the work of the enemy agent assigned to him. I wish I could see the feathered do gooder. I know the sneaky pest is there, but whenever I try to get a glimpse of him he sends off one of his rays of unbearable light. It hurts Dogwart. It burns and I don't like it. The unfeeling beasts resort to torture every chance they get. What makes it worse is that this patient could slip through my fingers at the last moment, and then what will happen to me? I'll be demoted and end up as a bus driver on one of those boring outings the Enemy allows all those who should be ours forever.

I took action. I found out that Mandible is in charge of that particular priest. Mandible is one of our most skilled agents. He told me that he keeps his patient totally booked up with administration, committee meetings and social engagements. My patient won't be able to see him for weeks. By then I should be able to solve the problem.

The patient's twinges also prompted the old goat to see the doctor, and the long and the short of it, dear boy, is that my patient has cancer. The trick now will be to keep him in a double bind. On the one hand I will make him obsessed with his health. Every twitch, pain or ache will be a sign that his cancer is getting worse. With any luck I will be able to get him signed up to see a long list of specialists, quacks and snake oil salesmen. (I like that 'snake oil' soubriquet don't you Dogwart? It has a certain *je ne sais quoi*.)

Every tactic will be to keep him thinking only of himself. At the same time I must make sure that he denies that there is anything wrong. Seeing him hop from one imaginary situation to the other will be very entertaining--rather like that game down below where we make the guests avoid the river of fire by hopping from one hot stone to another.

In this situation what you must not do is allow the patient to seriously and rationally consider that he might die. Their instinct to believe in their own immortality is one of their most ridiculous faults, and one to be encouraged. Should the patient calmly accept that he is going to die he will most certainly start to prepare for the occurrence. This not only means he will provide for his widow and family, but worst of all, he will make attempts to prepare his soul for death.

This is one of the hairless apes' most amusing foibles. They really do spend most of their lives blissfully unaware of Mr. Death. Every day they drive past graveyards and see ads for undertakers. Every day they see violent deaths reported on the news, and yet they still persuade themselves that the skull and crossbones don't apply to them. This happy trait is almost always to our advantage. If they continually deny the possibility of their own death, they deny even more energetically the possibility of what the enemy calls 'final death', or what our Father Below calls 'A Welcome Home'. As long as you can keep your patient in a state of denial about death you can lead him wherever you like.

We have contrived for the modern age to help us with this task in just about every way conceivable. In those terrible medieval times it was much more difficult. Everywhere a patient looked he saw death, disease and horror. The enemy's agents reminded them all the time that this life was a 'vale of tears' and that death would come soon, and that the time of their earthly life was to prepare for death. Happily all that is gone. It has been replaced with remorseless cheerfulness. Instead of the grinning death's head we have grinning presenters on television. Instead of grinning skulls we have grinning faces that have been lifted so many times that you can see the skulls underneath.

Instead of the enemy's awareness of death we have convinced the little apes that if they eat healthy food, have enough plastic surgery, diet correctly and exercise enough they will never grow old and die. As a result, all the time they might spend preparing for death and eternity, they spend trying to avoid death and eternity.

There is an especially delicious thrill when you get the timing right dear boy, and your patient meets the grim reaper in the midst of some desperate attempt to avoid the Grim Reaper. I had a patient collapse with a heart attack on a treadmill machine once, but my favorite case was the woman who was poisoned by her botox treatment. She wanted a facial expression of everlasting surprise, and by Lucifer, she got what she wanted.

Deleriously yours,

Slubgrip

WEEK THREE ~ *Tuesday*

Dogwart,

You told me that your patient dropped out of college and was feeling low because of a failed love affair. Have you done anything about this? Is he thinking about the girl all the time? Have you got him on the merry go round of 'what might have been' or 'what he should have said'? Have you brought this along into a nice low level resentment? It's only a short hop from there to proper hatred, and once you've got him into hating the girl in an obsessive way there are a multitude of delightful choices. Knowing you, dear boy, as I do, I daresay none of these possibilities have even occurred to you.

Have you done anything about the fact that your patient has got time on his hands? I hear that he has moved back home with his parents. That's good. You can make him feel inadequate and make them annoyed that he is turning into an unemployed freeloader. If possible, keep him unemployed. His parents will push him to get a job, but you must make him see that all the jobs out there are dull, uninteresting and beneath him. Tell him that he deserves an interesting, well paid post with little responsibility, but don't let him become aware that such posts do not exist anywhere.

He's at a loose end Dogwart, and what are you doing about it? This is just the sort of opportunity the enemy loves to use. You're so pleased that he is lying about watching daytime TV. Don't you realize that he will soon become bored, and when that happens he may start looking for something useful to do?

The best thing would be for him to find some appropriate friends to hang around with. Get in touch with Squirmtuggle. His patient went to high school with your patient. Squirmtuggle has succeeded in making his young man into a perfect scoundrel. His parents spoil him. He has also dropped out of college, and lives at home. He has his own car, access to his parents' beach house, a circle of good 'high-end' friends and a nice amount of disposable income. He is well spoken, good looking and charming. Furthermore, he has a secret drug habit which might be of use to you.

Honestly Dogwart, do I have to tell you everything? I would have thought you'd have been quick off the mark on this one, but you sit around gloating about the paltry successes and the fact that you are turning the lad into a couch potato. It's not really top notch tempting now is it?

Slubgrip

WEEK THREE ~ *Wednesday*

Dogwart,

It is sweet of you to keep asking about my patient, but may I remind you that I am the tutor and you are the trainee? It's not really your place to ask too many questions is it? It might come across as if you were information gathering with some sort of sinister intent, and that's not really the sort of impression we want to give now is it?

If you must know, my patient is feeling depressed and restless with the news of his cancer. He's pacing about like a trapped animal. Very nice indeed.

I hear that your boy attended the Friday evening Stations of the Cross last week. I expect that parochial vicar and his smarmy crowd were responsible for that invitation? What worries me is that you somehow 'forgot' to mention it to me in your last text. Did you think I wouldn't find out Dogwart? The problem is, you're lazy and overconfident. One or two little successes go to your head, and then you slack off. Dear boy, if you don't get off your fat backside it will soon be a rump roast.

Despite this setback let me encourage you. It is still early in Lent. Your patient has good intentions, but he will soon drift away. We've managed to get some very juicy television programs scheduled for Friday nights. Remind him about the 'reality TV' show where people are stranded on a desert island, but don't let him see that there is nothing 'real' about it. You can soon plant in his mind that it's beneficial psychologically and "far more real" than trooping around a church gazing at bad religious art and trying to feel sorry for a loser of a Jewish rabbi who was executed two thousand years ago.

If that young priest is inviting your patient to religious services, make yourself aware of what else is going on in that parish during Lent. Obviously the young priest has started up some devotions that I thought had died a death. Usually in that parish they confined their Lenten activities to 'justice and peace' meetings. A group of elderly people wearing sandals would meet in the parish hall and discuss environmental issues and third world debt, eat granola bars and drink organic carrot juice. Clearly that sort of thing is passé and this new breed of priest wants to bring back the traditional Catholic praying, bowing and scraping.

He has probably instituted something called 'Eucharistic Adoration.' What the sniveling apes do is worship the cookie they call 'Christ.' They kneel down before it, sing sentimental songs and shake incense at it. (How I hate those noxious fumes!) There are fewer more idiotic and disgusting practices in the whole world of religion. To my mind, Dogwart, it is downright obscene.

For a time we were winning the battle on this one. Catholics were putting their monstrances and humeral veils in mothballs. Groovy priests were doing 'relevant' liturgies instead. What a delight it was when the priests sat everyone in a circle and said, "Let us worship the Christ in one another!" and had everyone hug. Sadly the Enemy does not give up. Just when we thought we were winning, a new generation comes along and seems delighted with all the old Catholic customs. It makes me furious to see these new young priests don their chasubles and copes and bring out the incense. They pull in the young boys to be servers and now they're starting Youth Adoration Services!!

They're not to be tolerated! Smash them Dogwart. Do anything you can to make sure they fail. Tempt the sanctimonious creeps with all your might. Attack their ludicrous vow of celibacy. Push them into the muck and mire. Rub their noses in it.

Yrs,

Slubgrip

PS: My patient didn't sleep last night, and that is a worrying sign. Any change in circumstances, Dogwart, and the enemy jumps in and tries one of his tricks. Keep them dozy Dogwart—it's dull, but it's effective.

WEEK THREE ~ *Thursday*

My dear Dogwart,

The discovery that your patient attended the Lent Stations of the Cross last Friday forced me to acquire some extra information about what is going on. Britwiggle tells me he went to church with a Catholic girl who does 'pro-life' work. Where have you been you despicable worm? Where did he meet this nauseating little lipstick? Is she part of that young priest's God squad? How did you allow this to happen?

I expect it all took place while you and Squirmtuggle were chortling over your squalid little pornography success. You don't understand a thing do you Dogwart? Don't you realize that if the brutes meet a real girl who shines with what the enemy calls 'goodness' they will be smitten and instantly forget the smut they were looking at? This really is a disaster of the greatest magnitude.

I've checked the files. Your patient is of the emotional and romantic sort. He's going to be a sucker for a skirt--especially one with high ideals like this one. Furthermore, he's looking for a 'personal experience of his faith.' You should have kept him far, far away from any form of Christian community and directed his emotional, romantic nature into safer areas like literature, drama, film and music. We have enough servants in those fields to have kept him entertained for a very long time. If he had followed that path you could have led him very neatly into artistic or intellectual eccentricity, and that leads nicely into self centered decadence, and it is only a short hop from there to fully fledged doubt, cynicism, nihilism, and despair. I once led a young patient to commit suicide because he saw himself as a tragic poet who would die young.

Instead he is being drawn into a genuine romance and extra religious worship! Don't you see that there is a very real risk that your patient will experience some of the more disgusting aspects of the Catholic faith? Is this girl musical or artistic? Your patient may be introduced to Mozart or Palestrina or Bach. She may introduce him to Michelangelo, Caravaggio, Fra Angelico and the whole stinking army of Catholic artists and composers. Then where will you be? She'll probably get him to attend a "Solemn High Mass" performed by that weasel of a young priest. Then your man will start being interested in beautiful liturgy for hell's sake!

I'm afraid I do not have very high hopes for you Dogwart. Many more failures like this and I will have to make a report to the Undersecretary. I know what you need to do to get this fellow back on the broad downward path. You clearly need some assistance. I'm going to help out, but there will be a price to pay. My consultancy fees cost, shall we say, 'an arm and a leg.'

Yrs,

Slubgrip

WEEK THREE ~ *Friday*

Dogwart,

Learn from the master dear boy, learn from the master. How did I deal with my patient's sleeplessness? The old boy has the unfortunate habit of praying when he can't sleep. I didn't let him think of it. Instead I kept his mind on his pain. It was a delight to see him worry himself silly. I was tempted to scare him with a little thought of what awaits him below with us, but this is usually counterproductive. It makes them leap for the other side too quickly. So, dull as it is, I just kept up the gnawing cycle of worry.

It doesn't matter how you do it, but whenever you can, get the little worms to focus on themselves. Anything will do, get them to worry about the future or regret the past; get them to think what a victim they are, and how hard they have it. Whatever you do, don't allow them honest pleasures outside themselves. A walk in the woods, a ticket to the ballgame, a visit to an art gallery or even listening to music will direct them to something greater than themselves, and this is to be avoided. The enemy is sneaky dear boy. He will creep in under every disguise possible, and he'll use any kind of wholesome 'goodness' to draw the vermin into his net.

I shouldn't need to remind you that tonight that nauseating young priest is running Stations of the Cross again. I've gone the extra mile for you dear boy. I've got Flushtuggle and Trumpwiggle together. They have been very successful with two girls in your patient's parish. The girls are both young and pretty, but beneath their pretty skins and sweet smiles they'd give Cinderella's step sisters a run for their money. They're having a party tonight and have invited your patient. Make sure he goes to the party and does not go to Stations of the Cross.

I've also got in touch with Snoot. She's in charge of your young man's new female interest. Snoot's an expert in self righteousness and religious puritanism. It turns out the little lipstick in question is a bit of a snob. She went to a private high school, and is now enrolled in a very good Catholic girls' college. There's every possibility that she will look down on your patient, and not see him again. In fact, the girl is attracted to your little ape, but Snoot's got her thinking that he is an 'occasion of sin'. I had to chuckle when I found out. These female tempters are such professionals. Apparently Snoot has pulled this one off several times already: her female is actually sexually ignorant and scared to death of men, and Snoot has got her to hold her head high and has turned her virginity into the cause for a nicely developed sense of spiritual pride combined with prudery and old fashioned social snobbery.

I must go Dogwart. It's Friday and my sinuses are killing me.

Gloomily yours,

Slubgrip

WEEK THREE ~ *Saturday*

Dogwart,

How dare you attempt such a cheap trick! You reported to me that your patient went to the girls' party and you pretended it was a successful endeavor on your part, but my sources (no, I will not tell you who informed me) tell me that he only went to the party after the Stations of the Cross, that he stayed for an hour, drank only a couple of soft drinks and ate nothing. Why was the brat not eating anything on a Friday Dogwart? Was he fasting? Check this out Dogwart and report the full story to me. This is the constant frustration with this job: no one has any respect for their elders and betters. If I didn't have my network I would be constantly lied to, deceived and cheated.

Furthermore, both Flushtuggle and Trumpwiggle report that your patient was a total bore and engaged their girls in a serious conversation about the parish, telling them how "awesome" the young priest is. Happily both of the little trollops were bored out of their heads, and when they realized he wasn't responding to their flirtation, promptly dropped him. All in all, Dogwart, this has been a most unsuccessful outing.

When are you going to learn that tempting is not child's play? It is a serious business, and no one can tell what will happen next. The enemy's agents are all about us. They obscure their intentions in that blasted light of theirs and they always seem to be operating according to a set of rules I have yet to understand. Why is it that they so often laugh and sing when they are about their business? That's what I can't stand about them dear boy. They have no sense of dignity. They claim to be the enemy's higher creations, and yet they behave like children. Do you know a couple of them once played a practical joke on me? They got me to believe that my patient was about to throw himself from a bridge. As he went over I was, I admit, smiling with satisfaction. Then the wretched fellow bounced back up. It turned out he was wearing something called a bungee cord on his ankle and it was all a stunt.

I'm tapping this out late on Saturday, Dogwart. I am most displeased with you and after signing off I shall be filing my report with the Undersecretary. I'm not sparing you I'm afraid. You've had enough warnings. You deserve all you get, and I'm recommending that you be assigned to pitchfork duty in the circle of the heretics.

Slubgrip

WEEK FOUR ~ *Sunday*

Dogwart,

While you are on probation, waiting for news from below about your status, allow me to give you some instruction about your patient and the delicate matter of going to Mass. I know it is tiresome, and like you, there is nothing more dreary to my mind than when one's patient goes trooping off with all the other lemmings to engage in 'worship.' I have tried for centuries to understand what they see in it, but to no avail. A whole hour of gloomy music, a spiel by some pompous priest and then the long line while they all go up for their little holy snack. It bores me dear boy. It bores me to tears.

Nevertheless, duty is duty, and there are some things you can do to make the experience as meaningless as possible for your patient. First thing: make sure he doesn't plan ahead for Mass. Keep him in a muddle as to which Mass he will go to until the last minute. With any luck he'll forget entirely or else he will rush in at the last minute. Getting him to arrive late for mass is crucial. We don't want him to have time beforehand to sit in silence in the church. If he does this enough he might learn to really pray. The other good thing about getting him to arrive late is that it disturbs others. Get him to climb over other people after the service has started and to make as much noise as possible doing so. With a little bit of effort you will soon have him arriving late every week. Glimworm once had a man who trailed his whole family of eleven children into Mass exactly twelve minutes late every week. They disturbed the whole congregation by trooping down to the front like a second procession. Glimworm made sure it never occurred to the man that by moving the whole enterprise forward twenty minutes they could arrive on time with the same regularity.

I'm getting off track. Your second main task is to ensure that he gets nothing out of the so called 'Liturgy of the Word.' Never let him read the readings ahead of time, and make him overlook the fact that he can follow along with the readings with the booklet in the pew. Divert his attention Dogwart. It's easy to do. If possible get him to think negative things about his fellow worshippers. Point out that the old trout who gave him such bad marks in her English class is two pews in front. Remind him what a bad temper the man in the back row has.

If you can't get him to think negative thoughts just focus his attention on a pretty girl or even get him to make faces to entertain the children in front of him. Make sure he attends the Mass celebrated by his flaky parish priest. That way when the homily comes along it doesn't matter if he pays attention. It will most likely be on something like global warming or the need to be kind to puppies and kittens.

During the entire Mass try to cultivate in your patient a sense of impatience. Remind him how bored he is. If he is not bored, then get him to criticize the Mass. The music at his parish is genuinely awful. It won't be hard for you to get him to actually hate the old bat who strums that guitar and sings off key. Draw his attention to the way the altar servers slouch and pick their nose. Tell him that images like the sacred heart of Jesus are absurd and sentimental and tacky. Remind him how uncomfortable the pews are. You know the drill. Get on with it.

I personally can't stand being in the place after they take the collection. I find the atmosphere always becomes strangely uncomfortable after that. I haven't been able to pin it down, but I usually have to slip out for a breath of fresh air once the priest goes to the altar. I suspect you're the same, and if so, before you go make sure your patient does not go forward to receive the bread and wine. The best way to do this is to pump up one of his little sins in his imagination so that he thinks it is a mortal sin. They've been instructed not to go to communion if they are aware of a mortal sin in their life. Very few of them really understand what a mortal sin is, so you can inflate most anything to make them feel guilty enough to stay in their seats. Frizgiggle once kept a young woman from communion for ten years because she had taken a cookie without asking.

On the other hand, Dogwart (and I know this seems complicated) if you have managed to tempt your patient into serious wrongdoing, then you really should encourage him to go forward. The effects of receiving the bread and wine when the soul is in darkness actually works in our favor. If they continue down this road they will soon justify the sin they are committing and continue in it happily, never once thinking that their soul is in peril because they 'are faithful communicants.'

This tactic is especially encouraging of late dear boy. We've had abortionists, fornicators, adulterers, sodomites, lesbians, frauds, hypocrites, heretics and politicians sent down below because for years they received communion while in a state of mortal sin. All that time they really thought they had done nothing wrong. Even better, some of them received communion for years without believing anything at all simply because they were concerned about what others would think of them if they did not receive communion.

I tell you dear boy. The look of surprise on their faces was worth it all. There is nothing more delicious than to see the self righteous realize that they are headed for the barbecue. On the other hand, to see the surprise on the faces of the humble when they enter the other place is too terrible to describe.

Take these lessons to heart Dogwart. Perhaps they will sober you up after your recent fiasco at Friday night's party.

Slubgrip

WEEK FOUR ~ *Monday*

My Dear Dogwart,

May I congratulate you on your promotion! I never really intended to send that report to the undersecretary. I reconsidered and thought you deserved a second chance. You understand dear boy, that I was feeling a bit off. My head was simply splitting, and I was in somewhat of a dither over it all. Perhaps I was a touch irritable? I'm do hope you didn't take my tone too seriously. I was merely joshing with you; you know a bit of the old badinage! What's a bit of the old rough and tumble among friends? In fact, I feel very warmly toward you my boy.

Part of my harsh tone is down to the fact that I was misinformed. I perceived nothing but failure at the party on Friday evening. It is possible that the misinformation was intentional. I wouldn't put it past any of the skunks to be colluding together against me. I didn't realize that your patient came back to the party later, got himself drunk and actually had sexual relations with Trumpwiggle's gal. Good work! This is something to be rather satisfied about.

Do tell all the details. Did they 'go all the way' or was it just some heavy kissing and fiddling about with one another? I suppose I don't need to advise you to capitalize on his little adventure. Stay close to Trumpwiggle. Make sure she gets her gal to perceive the affair as 'true love.' This will help the girl to avoid the conclusion that she is a little slut, and take her down the road of fantasy romance instead. Your patient had the reputation of being a cold hearted prude. Tell Trumpwiggle to get the girl to be proud of 'getting him to bed.' Trumpwiggle's girl has succeeded where others have failed. Make sure the little strumpet feels proud of her conquest. Most of all, make sure Trumpwiggle encourages the girl to continue the relationship. If possible we want to produce a marriage based totally on lust. Nothing is more delightful than to see two of the bipeds come to loathe one another once their shallow lustful feelings have passed. There is little better than the despair they experience once they realize they are hitched for life to a dumb blonde or a thick hunk with whom they have nothing in common.

For your part, make sure your patient feels bad about what he has done. I hasten to add, he should not feel guilty because he has offended against the enemy. This might lead him to repentance and confession, which is something we do not want! Don't make him understand and accept his guilt, instead make him feel bad and ashamed of himself. It's not the same thing, but he doesn't realize that. He thinks the shame he feels is the same thing as guilt.

Don't let him focus on the objective wrong he has done. Instead focus his feelings on himself and on the girl. Make him sorry, not so much for what he's done, but what he's done to the girl. This will have the happy result of making him sorry not for what he's done, but the effect of what he's done. Keep him in the dark about the girl as much as possible. Trumpwiggle tells me she is quite the sexy little vixen, and has 'had' nearly a dozen men already. Don't let your patient figure this out, or he will write her off as a common slut and won't feel bad at all. Instead make him think she is a 'good Catholic girl'. If they 'went all the way' get him to worry that she may be pregnant. Before long he will be thinking of 'doing the right thing' and marrying the girl, and a little victory will become a great triumph.

As I was saying, you deserve the honor you will, no doubt, be receiving from our Father below. Well done! I only hope you will remember me fondly on your way down to give your report and undergo your examination. If you are invited to dinner with Undersecretary Knobswart do give the old fellow my best. At college I always predicted he would go far. (Careful not to call him 'Knobby' to his face. He doesn't like that from the juniors.)

You asked about me and my patient. Don't worry about us my dear fellow. We're chortling along quite happily. Nothing really to report on that front. All is well.

With fondest regards, your old friend,

Slubgrip

WEEK FOUR ~ *Tuesday*

Dogwart,

The news of your triumph at the party last Friday is simply all over the place. Your fame goes before you dear boy. Undersecretary Knobswart tells me you passed the exam in flying colors, and in a few days' time I will receive your medal of honor. I've been asked to host the dinner and make the presentation. You'll be the guest of honor dear boy. Do get your acceptance speech ready!

How I would have enjoyed helping you to further successes, but alas, I have had a note from Undersecretary Knobswart saying that our relationship is over, and you are to be transferred to my old friend Grimkin. He's a magnificent tempter Dogwart. You lucky devil! Grimkin is one of the old school, and will be able to help you consolidate your little triumph. Now that your patient has committed a really serious sin it will take all the skills of old Grimkin to help you make sure the pimpled youth moves from a brief lustful fling into that choice situation where he lives a life totally cut off from the enemy. Be sure you listen carefully to Grimkin. He likes to be shown the respect that is his due. A little admiration on your part will not go amiss, and dear Dogwart, please do not tease him about his bad breath. He's quite sensitive on matters like that and believe me, you will pay later.

Before you go to lower things, may I humbly offer you one more word of advice about your patient? If he has actually gone 'all the way' with the girl, then he has made a much deeper commitment than he realizes. The disgusting half-breeds like to think that what they do with their bodies doesn't really matter. He will, at one moment, try to imagine that what he did with the girl was 'just physical' and that it didn't really mean anything. In many cases this is to be encouraged because we can get them to indulge in all sorts of playful behavior that will bring them home to us while they imagine all along that 'it doesn't mean anything' or 'it was just a bit of fun.'

In your patient's case, however, you must encourage him to reject such thinking. Instead tell him that what he did really was meaningful. He's a religious boy, so this will fit with what he believes. Make him imagine that the sexual act on Friday night was serious business. In fact, tell him it was really the same thing as marrying the girl, and that he had better get on and 'make her an honest woman.' At very least he may start to think that in marrying he would be doing his duty, but with some gentle handling you will soon get him imagining that he is actually in love with her and that what happened on Friday was the beginning of a beautiful relationship. The trick, Dogwart, is to use their own beliefs against them whenever possible. He is right that the sexual act has deep meaning, and he understands enough of the enemy's design to know that what he did is really the act of a married person. If you can use that to lure him into a disastrous marriage you will seal your victory with true glory.

I must dash dear boy. My conservative Catholic patient is having pains in his side again. He's been worrying about the cancer for some time now, and I think he is due for a nice sharp stab of real fear. I think I'll wait until the wee hours of the morning. Then when he has one of his little pains I'll hit him with the sort of irrational fear of nothing at all that is so effective when they are vulnerable. I know I shouldn't take such pleasure is scaring them. It's below me—it's the past time of spooks, goblins and those sad creatures called ghosts, but it's amusing all the same.

I do hope you get on well with Grimkin dear boy. Stay in touch, and polish that acceptance speech for the awards dinner. It's going to be a fine night!

Yrs,

Slubgrip

WEEK FOUR ~ *Wednesday*

Dear Bracket,

I was delighted to receive Undersecretary Knobswart's letter confirming my new appointment as your guide and guardian. You will have heard that Dogwart has a new assignment, and you will be taking over his patient with me as your mentor.

It's sadly true that poor Dogwart was somewhat out of his league. He started playing with the big boys and couldn't keep up. Our Father Below has a very nice dictum which serves in such cases: 'Survival of the fittest' he always says. It's the best way to be fair don't you think? Those who are strongest, cleverest and most able to 'adapt' always come out on top, and that's as it should be. "Strive, Thrive and Survive!" as I always say. Dogwart simply wasn't in that category and he has been relieved of his duties. I hope I don't need to remind you that Dogwart himself is blissfully unaware of what is about to happen to him. He truly believes that he was summoned below to receive an award for his good work. Let's keep him in the dark about things for now shall we?

I must say, I've heard good things about you! At last the Undersecretary has sent me a tempter who is more of a colleague than a trainee. I can't tell you how tiresome is has been to have one mediocre student after another. They are lazy, ignorant and arrogant the lot of them. Not a few of them have attempted to undermine me, supplant me or badmouth me to the authorities below. I can tell from your paperwork that you are a class apart, and I feel honored to be assigned as your tutor. I hope you will consider me your friend as well as your mentor?

I see that you specialize in religious cases. Well done! I notice that you've had had some remarkable successes within the Anglican Church. You must me all about it. I've already heard how you turned a young clergyman right around through the old trick of ecclesiastical ambition. Did you take him down the obvious route of religious preferment? Did you work him into good jobs with the 'right people'--always introducing him to some of our choice people in high places until he would say most anything to impress them? It's a fine sight isn't it—seeing how they will eventually deny the faith and even support homosexual 'liberation' just to wear a pointy hat and live in a palace? Or did you go the other route and get him to reject all that pomp and finery and ambition (because he saw he would never become a bishop anyway) in order to start his own 'ministry' through which he gathered devotees, power and money? Either way is good dear boy, and I want to hear just how you did it.

I must warn you. You will have your work cut out for you with this patient of Dogwart's. It seems that he is actually more deeply religious than we first thought. He's definitely fallen into the wrong crowd, and Dogwart's failure is almost too much to countenance.

It's time for the emergency services, and I, for one, am glad you're here. Welcome aboard.

Yrs,

Slubgrip

WEEK FOUR ~ *Thursday*

To His Lowliness, Undersecretary Knobswart

Dear Undersecretary,

Thank you for your confidential report on Dogwart's 'examination' down below. I suspected as much, and will take suitable action with Grimkin.

Yrs,

Slubgrip

To: His Excellency Grimkin STD
Office of the Diabolical Council of Enquiries
Eighth Circle

My Dear Grimkin,

By now you will have made your first contact with my former protégé, Dogwart. Knobby has sent me the confidential report on Dogwart's examination during his recent visit below to receive his 'award.' I believe you have received a copy? Honestly, I don't know why these junior devils think they can pull the wool over the eyes of old Slubgrip. We've seen it all before Grimkin, and both you and I know that it simply doesn't pay to try to deceive one's superior.

I knew Dogwart was lying from the start about that little adventure last Friday night. Trying to deceive me was one thing, but the fact that he actually kept the lie going after he went below beggars belief. Didn't he know that our Lord Below maintains an intelligence network unimaginable in its beautiful complexity? Our Father may not know all, but he knows enough... Did you see the detail in Knobby's report that the pudgy little scamp was actually bragging about his accomplishments?

Yes, he did get his patient to return to the party and have a few drinks, but all the time he knew that the lad had done little more than kiss Trumpwiggle's girl and grope about a bit. Even the girl was disgusted with his amateurish performance. That Dogwart claimed this little outing as a triumph just goes to show how ridiculous he is. To tell you the truth Grimkin, I'm just a little insulted by the fact that they ever sent him to me in the first place.

To make matters worse, Knobby told me that the fat brat was spreading rumors about me down below. Said that he thought I "might be losing my grip", and that it was "very sad to see" that I was "struggling to stay on top of my patient with cancer." I knew the cretin was up to no good. It's lucky I've maintained my own network of informers.

Between you and me, I'm not much impressed with his replacement either. Bracket is a prissy young tempter, all brimstone smoke and filigree work. You should see the ornamentation he has on his wings! The leather has been worked into fine little arches and swirls, and I swear he's had his horns filed down professionally. He says he's an expert in theology and talks non-stop about something he claims is his own innovation. He loves to brag about his successes within Anglicanism. He says the priests of that church use all the traditional liturgical language, while not really believing any of it.

If it is true, it does sound rather splendid. For example, he says that Reverend Wooly says on Easter morning, "Today we celebrate the glorious resurrection of Our Lord Jesus Christ from the dead" but what he really believes is that "in some way I would wish to say that the teachings of Jesus continued to survive even after his tragic death." Another corker he told me concerned that dreadful girl from Nazareth called Mary. Bracket says the typical Anglican theologian will praise the enemy for the 'virgin birth' while what me means by that is not that the girl was a virgin when the enemy impregnated her, but that she conceived in the normal way, but that by 'virgin' he means she was a "specially pure and holy young woman."

He may be the one we need to pick up the pieces after Dogwart's debacle, but I doubt it. He's too refined. The patient needs someone with the rare combination of finesse and the ability to play rough if need be. Other than you dear Grimkin, the only one I could imagine would be a clone of myself. If only more tempters were like me, then we might just make some progress in this everlasting skirmish with the enemy.

Back to Dogwart: he suspects nothing Grimkin. Keep him locked in, and do as I have been doing and continue to feed him advice about how to handle his patient, then get him over here for the 'awards dinner' as soon as possible. Tomorrow night should be about right don't you think?

I'll prepare the marinade and the rotisserie. Will you bring along a couple of bottles of your red bile, Chez Napoleon?

Slubgrip

WEEK FOUR ~ *Friday*

Bracket,

I was totally intrigued to hear your account of theology within the Anglican clergy. I had no idea we had made such progress there! Here I was thinking it was just a bit of clerical ambition mixed up with the odd adventure with a choir boy, but you've done sterling work! I am full of admiration.

You're stepping into another league in the Catholic Church I'm afraid. Of course vast numbers of Catholics never take the faith seriously at all. We've had our successes here too my boy. You're not the only one to have tempted the clergy.

The one problem we have in the Catholic Church is that those who do take their religion seriously follow a religion that sets an impossibly high standard. Furthermore, the pious vermin really do believe that what they do matters eternally. You see the Protestants either believe the enemy will forgive everyone for everything (in which case it doesn't matter what you do) or they believe everyone is predestined to hell or heaven (in which case it doesn't matter what you do) Both groups have denied free will, which means they evidence a certain complacency and lukewarmness.

The Catholics who really believe what their church teaches, (and unfortunately since the publication of their boring little catechism there are more and more of them) really believe that they have been given free will by the enemy. I still have not been able to understand this fully, but it seems that they really do have a small measure of the enemy's ability to make choices. He also seems to honor their choices and he really gives them what they have chosen. Of course this works to our favor very frequently because they choose our way instead of his way, and our way leads very happily to family dinner at our place.

The disadvantage is that an increasing number take their choices seriously. They have a clear understanding that there is everything to play for, and that heaven or hell is their's for the choosing. This belief gives an edge to tempting Catholics that just doesn't exist within the other Christian churches. It means they are more alert. Too often they can see us coming. They are trained to take all sorts of preventative measures. The worst of them are aware every day that they are engaged in a spiritual battle, and they make absolutely the most awful patients.

I'm sorry to say that your new patient is becoming one of these. It is early days yet, and he is only just beginning to wake up to his full responsibilities, but his serious practice of Lent is an increasing problem, as is his developing friendship with the young parochial vicar and his crowd.

I hope you will not be offended if I offer you a few pointers from my own work with a patient who is a conservative Catholic? He is a man in his fifties well on the way to becoming a totally locked in hypocrite and pious fraud. You will have to look over my shoulder on this one Bracket, as my work with him is pretty much textbook stuff for Catholics.

Recently he's been experiencing some physical pains in his side and cancer was diagnosed. I've been getting him to be worried about it for some time, but I'll now switch over to get him into denial. If something is seriously wrong with him I don't want him to get spooked. Better that he should dismiss the pain, and tell himself that the doctor's diagnosis was wrong and that he probably only has heartburn. With any luck he will die in his present state of unrepentant hypocrisy and spiritual pride and we can then teach him the true definition of 'heart burn.'

Unfortunately, he bumped into his parish priest at the country club the other day. and spent a whole hour with him at the bar. I tried very hard to get my man to criticize the priest for being at the golf club at all, but to no avail. He actually likes his parish priest!

This is a great defeat for me. We are usually able to get the ultra conservative Catholics to criticize and disapprove of their priests. It's wonderful to see them meekly following brainless right wing politicians, or following some sort of conspiracy theory crackpot, all the time assuming that their priests are ignorant buffoons who have been taken in by some vast freemason conspiracy.

To make matters worse, the priest actually listened to my patient, bought him a drink and gave him some sensible advice. He told my patient to calm down and accept his fate. He said, "You're going to die sometime my son. If you are lucky enough to know when that might happen you'll be able to prepare for it. In the meantime what about a game of golf with me next Monday?" I tell you Bracket, it made my bile boil. The clear fresh air of common sense is like an icy blast to me. I hate it Bracket. It makes me shiver.

I've got to go. Dogwart's 'award dinner' is tonight and I must sharpen the cutlery. I'm sorry we couldn't manage an invitation for you, but high table is full, and although Dogwart was nicely plump, he wasn't really that large. I'll try my hardest next time an award dinner comes up to invite you my dear fellow.

Yrs,

Slubgrip

WEEK FOUR ~ *Saturday*

Bracket,

The award dinner last night was splendid. Nothing like a few old friends gathered around the table. Grimkin was in good form, and told a rollicking story about how he once got a famous evangelical television preacher into a hotel room with a prostitute. When the TV crews arrived he claimed he was 'ministering' to her. Grimkin said it gave a whole new definition to 'the laying on of hands.'

Snozzle was there as well as Britwiggle and Crasston. Despite my hospitality, Corpulous, who was serving the table, told me that Crasston and Snozzle were bad mouthing me and planning a false report on me to Knobswart. They will soon find out that it doesn't pay to undermine Slubgrip. I haven't made it to my present position through charm alone.

Enough unpleasantness my dear fellow. I want to congratulate you on your first success with your patient. Last evening he could have gone to Stations of the Cross, and he may very well have gone to confession and cleared up that matter of his sexual peccadillo last Friday evening. You were very clever to work with Trumpwiggle to get the boy back together with the girl last night. You are quite correct that it would have been a crude failure to get the two of them back into each other's arms so soon.

You and Trumpwiggle did well to get them engaged in that serious discussion so full of psycho babble. Did Trumpwiggle's girl really say she 'gets involved sexually because her father doesn't love her enough?' She probably picked that up in one those teen magazines she devours. I enjoyed your report that your patient listened to her and agreed with all her shallow excuses. Keep working on this one Bracket. Once they both believe that they are victims they might just go to bed together in the belief that they need to 'comfort' one another.

You might just get them together this evening. Trumpwiggle will get the girl to appeal to your patient's sympathy. If she calls or emails, and sounds pitifully lonely he'll probably respond, and who knows, they might go out together. Keep up the subtle work. Don't let them have much physical contact. Better to keep that on a low boil for now in order to build up a 'relationship' that will eventually pay dividends. Even if they just stay out late, you will probably be able to get your patient to sleep in and miss Mass tomorrow.

On your toes Bracket! Keep up the good work.

Slubgrip

WEEK FIVE ~ *Sunday*

My Dear Grimkin,

It was a delight to have you to dinner on Friday. Getting Dogwart to dress up in the uniform of the Legion of Honor, complete with the frock coat and pomade hat was hilarious. I'm glad you enjoyed my menus with Dogwart's name as the main course. He hadn't a clue what was going on, and the look on his face when he read the menu was unforgettable. I thought I would never stop laughing when, during my after dinner speech I wondered how Dogwart would enjoy the nether regions and you blurted out, "He'll have to make it through my nether regions first...."

Grimkin, you are probably wondering why I invited Crasston and Snozzle to our dinner the other night. The truth is, I am constantly on the lookout for loyal informers at every level. Information is power Grimkin, and to stay on top we need to know what's going on below us. I'm convinced that Corpulous and Britwiggle are loyal, but Crasston and Snozzle are newly transferred, and I've been hearing some rumblings from them. Crasston is sixth degree, and has been looking for promotion for several centuries now.

My people tell me that Snozzle was transferred here for gross misconduct. He allowed a patient whom he had control of for years, to see a Catholic priest on his deathbed, and before Snozzle could do anything the fellow had 'confessed' his sins, received the 'sacrament' and slipped through Snozzle's claws. Anyway, Snozzle is feeling sore about his demotion, and I suspect he and Crasston are plotting to reveal some lies about me to Knobby. My suspicions proved correct. Britwiggle and Corpulous ingratiated themselves and after a few too many glasses of your excellent Chez Napoleon Crasston and Snozzle started talking.

They are trying to dig up my old 'problems' and make a mountain out of a molehill. I suspect there's nothing the two of them would like better than to step into our shoes Grimkin, and I hope you'll help me keep an eye on them.

Really Grimkin, the deceit and plotting that goes on around here is quite tiresome. If only such things as the enemy's foolish ideals of 'honesty' and 'fair play' and 'loyalty' really existed, life would be ever so much easier.

Anyway, enough grumbling, chin up and remember the old school motto: Live to Burn, Burn to Live.

Slubgrip

WEEK FIVE ~ *Monday*

Dear Bracket,

I have to report something about my own patient for your instruction. He has agreed to attend a Healing Mass. It happened like this: First my patient was playing the back nine with his priest, and the next thing I know they're in the clubhouse knocking back a couple of whiskeys. Knowing the priest's fondness for the nectar of Scotland, I admit I dozed off for a few moments. The enemy saw the gap and was through it in a flash. He used the booze to lower my patient's resistance. Imagine the sneakiness of it! Next thing I know the priest has brought up the topic of this healing Mass, and my patient has signed up.

I am not making excuses Bracket --just explaining so that you might learn from my mistakes. I'm sure there is nothing to be too worried about. I have been working on my conservative Catholic patient now for many years. I've groomed his taste for things old fashioned so that he now confuses his sentimental attachment to the Middle Ages with doctrinal orthodoxy and the heights of spirituality.

The poor booby actually thinks that he is closer to God because he loves the Latin Mass, fiddleback chasubles, incense and lacy vestments. I agree with you Dogwart that such things are hideous, but I would rather have my patient attached to them and be truly uncharitable to everyone he disagrees with than to be open minded and patient. I once had him engage in an email debate for three weeks on whether a lay person was allowed to touch the ciborium without wearing white gloves. If only you could see my moments of triumph!

I must get back to the point. The healing Mass is taking place in the neighboring parish where the church looks like a huge brick dunce cap. Because of all my work over the years, my patient hates the place. I'll try to get him to cancel, but if he gets through the door and takes one look at the priest's day-glo vestments and hears guitars and sees all the happy people in jeans and T-shirts hugging one another he is likely to gag and run for the door. He's a snob Bracket! a snob of the most deliciously religious type! I doubt whether he'll even get past the holy water stoop, but it is still a dangerous proposition. I'll have to stick by him. You work and work for years, and then one little cancer scare and they become intractable and unpredictable.

I'll keep you posted,

Slubgrip

WEEK FIVE ~ *Tuesday*

Dear Bracket,

I hardly dare to write to you on the subject of prayer, as you are already such an experienced tempter. Your achievements amongst the Anglican clergy are truly astounding, and I feel sometimes that you ought to be my teacher, instead of me instructing you! If what I say is old hat, please disregard it completely and forgive an old fool like myself for even presuming to instruct you. Humor me if you must Bracket, but I would not be doing my job if I didn't remind you of a few pointers in this most difficult area.

From what you've said, your boy's recent dalliance has made him rather serious, and with the present company he is keeping, no doubt he will start to take prayer more seriously. Whenever I have found myself in this situation, I've relied on the basics, and usually one doesn't need to take any further steps. You may remember from Knobby's course that the very first step is to keep your patient in an infantile state of mind about prayer.

He was taught to say certain sentimental childish prayers before going to bed. Don't let him learn any others. Keep his prayer life on the level of bedtime stories, cuddles from Mummy and Winnie the Pooh. As a result he will equate prayer with asking Santa Claus for toys at Christmas, the tooth fairy and the Easter Bunny. With any luck his faith will stay totally at that level. A nice side effect of this tactic is that he will put all the Bible stories he learned into the same mental category of fairy tales and children's fantasy. After all, the story of David and Goliath isn't that different from Jack and the Beanstalk, and the story of Mary and the Angel Gabriel is rather like Cinderella and her fairy Godmother.

You really needn't do much at all for this to happen. It is the default setting for most people who have had a religious upbringing. If he should start to take prayer seriously all you need to do is remind him of asking Santa for things at Christmas, and he will immediately think that prayer is the same sort of 'magic' and that it is only for babies, and doesn't work.

It may be, however, that your patient does begin to take prayer more seriously. He may start to ask all the obvious questions, "How does God hear everyone's prayer at the same time?" or "How can God answer prayer if different people ask for different things?" Keep him at that level and he will soon see just how absurd the whole notion of prayer really is. What he mustn't do is persist in questions about prayer, because if he has any intelligence at all he will soon see that his first questions were infantile, and he may start asking better questions about prayer, and when he does that you will find your man beginning to get into trouble.

Keep him from reading any books on prayer. They will not only take his infantile questions seriously, but they will attempt to provide sensible answers. They will offer smug little aphorisms like, "Prayer doesn't change God, it changes you", or "The reason God can answer everyone's prayer is that he says the same thing to everyone." It's amazing how the cretins gobble up these inane answers. The problem is, Bracket, they actually want to believe in prayer. They have this strange desire for prayer to really work and be meaningful. It's simply a rather pitiful wish to be significant. They want to think God is on their side, and that they have friends in high places.

I need to go. My patient has stopped feeling sorry for himself and has decided to go to the theater with his wife. I wish I could rely on him to make a good choice, but I'm going to have to traipse along. The enemy is attacking him quite regularly these days, and I can't let up even for a moment.

I will write more about prayer tomorrow. In the meantime, try to get the boy to go out with Trumpwiggle's girl again this evening.

Yrs,

Slubgrip

WEEK FIVE ~ *Wednesday*

Dear Bracket,

Delighted to hear that your patient and Trumpwiggle's gal got together last evening again, and that he is feeling sorry for her. Keep him involved with her and make sure he doesn't think of that other do goody little lipstick of Snoot's. Just between you and me Bracket, Snoot brags about her accomplishments with goody two shoes types of girls, but to tell you the truth, she's let one or two slip through her fingers. One ended up as a perfectly horrible nursing sister in Calcutta and the other married a hearty Catholic man, had a rip roaring love life and produced thirteen children. It makes me spit bile just thinking about it!

Bracket, bear with me while I say one or two other things about prayer. Your young man might stop thinking about prayer and simply start praying. Do everything you can to interrupt this. Bring other thoughts into his head. Simpletons like Dogwart try to put lustful thoughts there, but it rarely works. The enemy agents help the little hairless apes to see your trick and sidestep. My advice is, don't bother with all that. Instead get him thinking about the work he has to do, the plans he has for the future, what is for supper and whether or not he remembered to take out the trash. Before long he'll give up, get up and start something else.

If he does start praying it won't be long before he runs out of ideas.

Unfortunately Catholics have dozens of ways of praying. Their odious 'saints' have experimented with many different forms of prayer. I suggest you resort to the Infernal Encyclopedia to brush up on all these tiresome habits, but I should warn you of one form that is especially noxious. The priests have something called 'The Liturgy of the Hours'. This is an ancient collection of prayers, hymns and readings from their favorite authors. It is a most revolting collection of sentimental nonsense, archaic fol-do-rol and obtuse theological clap trap. The vast majority of the stuff is no more than second rate, out dated Hebrew poetry. (How I hate that swarthy race of brutes. If only our German servants in the last century had finished the job!)

You must never let your patient get started with what is called liturgical prayer. If he does he will have to develop discipline, expand his mind and learn to like something greater than himself. This in itself is bad enough, but that he should do so through the words and thoughts of the Enemy's greatest agents is unthinkable. The other danger is that he will turn to a source outside himself for the words of prayer. This is to be avoided at all costs. You do not want him to find an objective ground for his faith. Keep him focused on his own feelings and thoughts.

If that young priest tries to get your patient interested, make sure the words 'Liturgy of the Hours' sounds arcane, antique and medieval to him. (and by the way, make sure the word 'medieval' is synonymous with torture, plague and 'the Dark Ages')

If he should open one of the books make sure it is the biggest. Direct him to a four volume set with lots of colored ribbons. Make him think that he would never learn how to use such a vast and daunting collection of books. Remind him that such 'prayer' is boring and that 'real' prayer is 'just talking to the Lord'. As long as he is only using his own banal words and thoughts he is unlikely to do more than talk to himself, all along thinking that he is talking to God. With any luck you will be able to keep him in this mode of 'prayer' until he really believes that in talking to himself he is talking to God. This is one of the neatest ways to make your patient believe he is God without ever realizing it.

The long and the short of it is, your patient may start to pray. We know that 'prayer' is really just an elaborate form of wishful thinking and self deception, but the problem is, the humans really do believe they are in touch with the enemy. I know what you're thinking: "If there is nothing to it, why be so worried that they might learn how to pray?"

It's because they go on from praying to become quite insufferable little brutes, that's why. Some sort of process goes on that our best researchers are still unable to explain. Prayer transforms them. All I can say is that when they start to pray they move away from us. They become distant and difficult to get to. Then the enemy agents step in and throw up their stupid shield of light and you know how that burns and blinds you.

I'm getting quite sick just thinking about it. Be on your guard Bracket.

Yrs,

Slubgrip

WEEK FIVE ~ *Thursday*

My Dear Bracket,

I know it is in poor taste to boast, but really, I must tell you something that has happened that is quite wonderful. Of course I relate this for your own education. We must learn from one another dear boy. In due time I want to learn more of your tactics with the Anglican clergy, but for now you really must hear what happened last night with my own patient.

You may recall that his cancer has frightened him enough to talk to his parish priest, and that the old fraud seriously suggested that my patient attend the healing Mass at the neighboring parish. Well, my dear, this parish church looks like a cross between a parking garage and a flying saucer, and my conservative Catholic patient hates it. Nevertheless he discovered that the healing Mass was last night, and just when I thought they were going off to the cinema, his wife convinced him to change plans and they went to the healing Mass.

I'm relating this story so you can learn from the Master dear boy. Perhaps you would have done anything possible to keep him away from a healing Mass. The fact of the matter is, some of these more informal Catholics do seem to have some sort of special contact with the enemy. The enemy's agents flock about these meetings like a gaggle of geese. If you've been to one of these meetings you'll know what I mean. The light is almost unbearable, and the sickly "praise and worship songs" combined with everyone pretending to be happy in Jesus is enough to drive the most experienced of us out into the night in a howling fit.

Despite all this I allowed my patient to attend the healing Mass.

I know my man, and have been working a long time to achieve the stunning result last night. My patient went in with his wife and sat at the back. Immediately all my long years of training paid off. He went into attack mode. When the music started up he shook with rage at the nightclub style and greeting card lyrics. When he saw the altar servers wearing shapeless white robes instead of black cassocks with white surplices he was indignant.

Then when he spotted that one of the servers was not only female, but was wearing high heels his temperature went up another notch. I then pointed out six or seven minor liturgical abuses, helped him see that the priest's homily was not only sentimental, but that it veered rather closely to Protestant heresy by emphasizing the need for personal faith. By the time the syrupy healing music was under way my man was more willing to join us below than to stay there and go forward for the laying on of hands and "healing." He walked out simmering with rage and for the rest of the evening stayed in a nice stew of spiritual state of hatred, hypocrisy and self righteousness

Bracket, I only hope that you ascend to such heights as I have last night. It is a true joy to see the fruit of your hard labors after so long. One day you may find yourself in a senior position similar to my own, and I wish you will enjoy the benefits as much as I have. It is a truly glorious moment for me Bracket, and I don't mind sharing it with you.

Deleriously yours,

Slubgrip

WEEK FIVE ~ *Friday*

To: His Excellency Sub Tempter Grimkin
Office of the Diabolical Council of Enquiries
Eighth Circle

Grimkin,

I was astonished to receive your message. I'm not surprised that Crasston and Snozzle have been to you with a complaint against me, but I am surprised that you entertained their wild story even for a moment.

Grimkin, we are friends from college days. Do I need to remind you of the time I lied to rescue you from Knobby's pitchfork? Don't you remember our first patients? You were so successful at keeping that old widower in a state of despair, and you helped me keep that miserly banker locked in his greed. Those memories are sweet Grimkin, and when the banker and the widower went down, and we got our first ruby coals on our epaulets don't you remember our victory drink? After all we've been through, how can you write to me in such a tone?

I'm not going to insult our friendship by taking your questions seriously. Allow me to simply repudiate totally the charges the Crasston and Snozzle have put. They are unscrupulous climbers Grimkin. They are ambitious liars, and we both know it. I'm hurt that you even took them seriously, and appeal to you to place the file exactly where it belongs: in the flames.

Let's forget all about it dear Grimkin. I won't hold it against you. Why not come around here tomorrow evening and we'll dine. I've prepared a particularly nice pair of adulterers in a sweet sour sauce, followed by a fine haunch of murderer for the main course and a delicate pastry filled with hypocrites. I've got a couple of bottles of black and yellow bile. Just bring yourself Grimkin, and we'll bury the hatchet.

Your old friend,

Slubgrip

Corpulous,

I write in haste. Snozzle and Crasston have been snitching on us to Grimkin. Get the sneaks before it's too late. Hurt them Corpulous. Take Cerberus with you. Teach them a lesson. Do it now.

Slubgrip

Britwiggle,

I'll come straight to the point. Did you know that Crasston and Snozzle have it in for you? I've been told by two different sources that they have reported you to Knobby for planning a coup at the office of the Undersecretary for Feminine Temptation, and a copy has gone to Grimkin.

The time has come for you to do what I told you to do. Don't delay. I need all the help I can get at the moment dear girl. I'm depending on you. My head is splitting. You must help old Slubgrip, and remember no risk, no reward, and in this case the rewards will be rich and the rewards will be shared!

Yr Slubgrip

WEEK FIVE ~ *Saturday*

Bracket,

Glimtongue, who is in charge of that young priest, tells me that your patient has been to confession. I should have known that you would keep it secret, and that I would have to rely on my network of intelligence gatherers. I hope you are not going down the same road as poor Dogwart!

Why, oh why, does a tempter of your stature not have the wit and shrewdness to come clean when something goes wrong? My dear boy, don't you understand that I am on your side! We all make mistakes and had you come to me immediately we could have worked together to put things right. Didn't you know that I would find out anyway?

I also understand that your patient got together with Trumpwiggle's gal again on Friday, and that she seduced him. Is that why the little worm went to confession on Saturday? You should have seen it coming and told Trumpwiggle to restrain her girl a bit. The two of you overplayed your hand, and now all may be lost (including the fine filigree on your wings you pathetic poseur)

I shouldn't need to tell a tempter of your reputation that you should not let them even get close to the idea that they ought to make their confession. It doesn't matter that they don't really understand what is going on. The worst thing about confession is that the little rodents get down on their knees and squeak out their sorrow for their paltry little sins, and that they feel so ashamed of squalid, insignificant little misdemeanors. At the heart of the degrading habit is that they are humbled by the experience. They soon bounce back to their usual self centredness, but even one moment of genuine humility stinks Bracket. It smells sickly sweet and makes me quite ill.

Keep them away from the confessional! I cannot stress it enough. There are a multitude of ways to do this. Here is one: Tell them that things they have done are not so bad. If they see their faults get them to say to themselves, 'Well, I'm only human.' This is an especially delicious form of pride because it seems to the patient that instead of being arrogant and proud they are actually being down to earth and homely. By saying, "Well, I'm only human," they will feel even more proud of themselves for being just an 'ordinary Joe or Jane.'

If you can do that they will not only retain the sins that will lead them to our eternal home, but they will come there in a state of blissfully ignorant self righteousness--firmly believing in their own simple down to earth goodness--never once suspecting that they are nearly as proud as our Father Below.

A ploy which is almost exactly the opposite works just as well. Instead of diminishing what they have done with "Well, I'm only human after all." Get them to imagine that what they have done is cosmic in its wickedness. Get them to say to themselves, "What I've done is so terrible that no one can forgive me", then keep them from the confessional because of their belief.

Once you've kept them from the confessional you must remind them that they also mustn't go to receive their blessed bread and wine since they have done such a serious sin. It doesn't matter if what they've done is insignificant. In fact, if it is insignificant the trick is even more entertaining. I once had a woman stay away from confession and communion for five years because she had taken a pencil home from the office.

If they do go into the confessional, make sure they focus on the sins of which they are most ashamed. These will invariably be the sins of the flesh. The hairless apes are actually very prudish about their bodies, and sins they feel most ashamed of are sins that involve the area below the belt. Encourage this. Make them feel that these sins of the flesh are the most terrible and heinous crimes. With just a little bit of skill they will neglect to mention that they have eaten and drunk too much, been lazy, lied, cheated, been envious, gossiped, used verbal violence and lived lives of total selfishness.

Your patient may have gone to confession, but you should be able to keep him out of the horrid cupboard in the future. Just tell him that Catholics don't have to go to a priest to confess. Tell him it is just as effective to say he's sorry to God on his own. Tell him that this is actually better since he can do it instantly after he sins, and besides "the priests are all so busy!" Never let him see that only the priest can grant him 'absolution', and that without the priest it is not a sacrament at all. Neither should you let him see that saying 'sorry to God' on his own is a rather cowardly option.

Snoot tells me that her girl has been difficult and has been showing interest in your patient. Has there been contact between them? This is not good Bracket. Furthermore, as your patient went to that young priest for confession he will probably give him a penance that will throw all our plans into a tailspin. What if the priest told the boy to dump Trumpwiggle's girl?

I have tried to help you Bracket, but I can't protect you from your own ineptitude. When Knobby's boys come for you in the Black Widow don't expect me to stick up for you.

Yrs,

Slubgrip

WEEK SIX ~ *Sunday*

Bracket,

Thank you for your kind words about my own patient, but don't imagine that flattery will get you back in my good books. We want results Bracket, not smooth talk. But yes, I must admit, the incident at the healing Mass was gratifying indeed. There are times when it all 'comes together' and this was one of them. The old timers speak of the 'warfare' they once engaged in with the enemy's agents; well I can tell you Bracket, the enemy agents were out in force that night. The air was thick with the stench of them, but I came through with flying colors, and it was all the more pleasing for the fact that it was not a sudden victory, but the result of years of hard, patient and careful work with my patient. You are right that it could have been a disaster. What if he had gone forward to receive 'healing prayer'?

Let me tell you what it was like Bracket. The sister and the priest who were visiting the parish were being swarmed by the enemy agents. They were surrounded with them like a mob of excited teenage girls at a rock concert. It was quite sickening. They were laying hands on people and praying over them in an embarrassing fashion. Individuals were weeping and repenting of their 'sins'. The humans were crooning awful sentimental songs about the 'Holy Spirit' and pleading to be 'melted, made and molded.' I didn't know whether to laugh or run howling from the hullabaloo. Bracket, it makes me cringe just telling you about it. Very distasteful dear boy, very distasteful indeed!

Happily, my patient was just as disgusted by the display as I was, and he and his wife made a hasty exit. Meantime, it looks like your own patient is getting more interested in his religion, and that he is falling under the spell of that young traditionalist priest.

If he must get involved with such a boring group of goody goodies, then make sure he becomes passionate about their particular form of worship. Make sure he focuses exclusively on the form of religion and misses the heart of it all. It has worked nicely with my own conservative Catholic patient, and there is no reason why the formula can't work for your young man as well. Let him read books that praise the traditional mass and criticize the new order of the Mass. Get him involved with one of those sour, paranoid ultra traditionalist groups if you can. They're bound to do half of your work for you, and with a little luck you can turn him into a negative, self righteous, puritanical young priest who will not only be on an express train to our mansions below, but will succeed in bringing lots of others with him.

Your boy is a sentimentalist at heart, so it may be that he is just as susceptible to extremes of charismatic worship. If the ultra traditional Catholics are all rules, regulations and no heart, the extreme charismatics are all heart with no form. If your patient is attracted to the charismatic style, play it up and get him to join a far out charismatic Catholic commune. With any luck he'll end up in one of those cults where they all drink poison while they wait for the angels to come for them.

Whatever course you take, makes sure it is not only extreme, but exclusive and negative towards everyone else. What you must avoid at all costs is a religious commitment that is steady, realistic, good humored and genuinely open minded and tolerant of others. If you must, get him all wrapped up in religion, but do not let him get wrapped up in what the enemy calls 'the life of faith.' This is a form of life in which the patient really is curious, open and ready to learn new things.

Our researchers are still trying to understand this strange manner of life that some of the humans seem to attain. It is as if the form of their religion is secondary to some relationship they have with another person or entity. These types always keep us guessing. They're hard to pin down. As soon as you think you've got them wrapped up in a sentimental charismatic sect they drop it and start attending a Latin Mass. As soon as you think they are obsessed by Latin liturgy and moral theology, they surprise you with what seems to be genuine tolerance and a sense of humor. These human beings are a threat Bracket. They seem to use all the forms of religion, without being fanatical about any of them.

The worst ones are those who profess to be 'ordinary Catholics.' Their open curiosity is guided and informed by their church's teachings, so it is almost impossible to get them sidelined into some extremist group. They obey the church's teaching, but the have a strange way of looking beyond it to something else. It is as if they regard the rules, rubrics and regulations of religion as tools to be used, or a ladder to climb on.

They seem to have integrated religion with every aspect of their life, and if you are not alert you would think they were not religious at all. In fact, they are often very difficult to spot. They are not necessarily very pious, in fact they may appear to be very ordinary mortals. Because they don't take themselves seriously they blend in. What you want to look out for is something the enemy calls 'joy'. This unpleasant trait looks like ordinary happiness, but it runs deeper in them. It is marked by a certain freedom and sense of humor. Watch out for these types! They are dangerous Bracket, very dangerous! I must admit, these types frighten me. I can't figure them out, and the only conclusion I can draw is that they are seriously deranged in some way. Avoid them Bracket, and make sure your patient avoids them too.

Yrs,

Slubgrip

WEEK SIX ~ *Monday*

My Dear Snoot,

Bracket tells me that yesterday at Mass his patient just happened to 'bump into' your girl. This won't do. Are you not aware of the fact that Trumpwiggle and I have been working very hard to help Bracket with his patient? We were making very good progress, and I was counting on you to do your part.

Snooty, my dear, you don't know how often I've bragged on you as being one of the very best in the business. You are so cool, so professional, so very 'top drawer'. Your ability to lure females into various delightful roles is second to none. You have an instinct my dear. Whether it is the 'society sweetheart', the Hollywood star, or the 'femme fatale' you groom the human females with great finesse. I've seen you take a very ordinary looking waif and turn her into a sultry, slinky model who believes herself to be a kind of goddess. Likewise, you've been able to transform a simple high school girl into a flirt and tease, all the time showing them how wonderful they are, you have kept from them their own vanity, cruelty and delightful egomania.

How then, could you let us down so badly? You told me you had the girl believing that Bracket's patient was 'an occasion to sin' and 'a bad influence'. You assured me that she was coming along nicely as a puritanical, prissy prima donna, and you let her meet the boy at Mass? Bracket thinks the girl sat near him at Mass on purpose. He says she paid no attention to what was going on in church and was constantly trying to catch the boy's eye, and that it was all Bracket could do to keep the boy praying as the lesser of two evils. This was the sticky situation you got Bracket into: should his patient pray or should he distract the boy from praying to play googly eyes with your girl?

Luckily Bracket has a good head on his shoulders and he realized that, in the long run, a few moments in prayer would be better than a lifetime with your girl, who is not only well in with the enemy, but comes from a strong and happy Catholic family.

Hells bells girl! Keep your little saint away from Bracket's boy! She stinks Snooty. I don't want her anywhere near the lad. Can't you see what might happen? If he falls for her (and she's just the sort he would fall for) they might end up producing another whole litter of repulsive Catholic babies. I hate it Snoot. I hate the way the enemy uses the disgusting physical brutes to manufacture more and more half breeds.

Keep her away my girl, or you'll soon find your high class made up face is back in the circus where it belongs.

Of course, I say this for your own good my dear,

You know how I adore you, and always have.

Slubgrip

WEEK SIX ~ *Tuesday*

Bracket,

My dear fellow, I thought better of you. Is it true that your patient not only went to confession on Saturday, but attended the young priest's Bible study last night, and that Snoot's girl was there and the two of them sat together? Lucifer below Bracket! Don't you understand that a boy and girl actually enjoying religion together is just about the worst possible scenario?

At least we don't have to worry too much about the Bible study part of it. We've been extremely successful over the last two hundred years in this area. Our agents in Germany began with the Protestant scholars by getting them to question the historicity of the Bible. They soon got to work with their usual Teutonic efficiency, first killing and then dissecting, and before long they doubted everything they read in the Bible. If something could be disproved historically or scientifically it was considered to be spiritually and morally dubious as well. It never occurred to most of them that they were mis-reading the whole intention of the book they were studying. When they found that the Scriptures were not primarily a historical record or a scientific textbook their response was like the dunderhead who is angry because the telephone directory doesn't have a good plot.

Rather than drawing the obvious conclusion that the Scriptures were primarily a religious book, we helped the Biblical scholars to understand that all the religious elements were 'later interpolations' by the 'early Christian community.' The assumption was that this was therefore somehow dishonest. With very little effort therefore, we got them to dismiss both the historical and literal understanding of the Scriptures as well as the religious. All of this was done with various forms of 'higher criticism.' (Notice how we called it 'higher' criticism, when in fact it was a much more literal and therefore 'lower' form of thought--our father thought of that sleight of hand.) The literary critics, redaction critics, historical critics all had their day.

Most of them had lost what faith they had before they even started, and it was a joy to watch them proceed with 'objective research' and publish their 'results of unbiased scholarship', when in fact, their hearts and minds had long been closed to anything but their own careers, and what careers we gave them for their work! They were feted by the academic establishment, granted awards at the highest level, had rich academic careers in the juiciest of universities and lived very well off their work.

Now our work is almost complete. You see, Bracket, the real aim of all the various forms of criticism was not just to undermine the authority of the enemy's horrid book of fairy tales, but to throw up endless clouds of disagreement and division in the enemy's ranks. In the end none of the scholars (or their groups of devotees) could agree about anything, so they all agreed to disagree. As a result we have been able to replace the enemy's once solid foundations with quicksand. The Bible now means whatever anyone wants it to mean.

Do you see how the seed for this was planted hundreds of years ago? It all started by putting the idea into that fellow Luther's head that the Scriptures were to be the only rule for Christian belief and life. This little half truth sounded so good at the time that it was hard to resist, but through it we now have the Protestants believing whatever they like, and going through the Bible to find support for it.

If they don't like what they find in the Scriptures the 'higher criticism' allows them to dismiss a text because it 'is not found in the earliest manuscripts' or because 'scholars are not sure if St Paul really wrote that passage' or 'we know that this passage is to be interpreted metaphorically and not to be taken literally.'

A particularly sweet example of this complete relativism occurred in England not too long ago. One of our agents named Pertwee, was recently promoted to the highest levels because of the long term plan he put into effect. A recent Archbishop of Canterbury named John Carew argued for women priests. (actually Mrs. Carew was the enthusiastic one, but that's another story) and when opponents pointed out that women's ordination went against Scripture, Carew said that those passages may not have been written by St Paul, and "we now know more about men and women's roles than they did in the first century."

Once women priests were ordained, the homosexualists started campaigning for equal rights, and when Carew resisted this innovation because it was against Scripture the homosexualists said, "It's not certain that St Paul wrote those passages, and besides, we know much more about human sexuality now than they did in the first century." Poor old Carew's face was a picture of befuddlement, and the hoots and catcalls from the galleries below were enough to win old Pertwee a place at high table.

That's enough for now,

Slubgrip

WEEK SIX ~ *Wednesday*

Bracket,

Yesterday I was discussing the problem of your patient's attendance at a parish Bible study. Because he is a Catholic there are certain aspects to this disturbing problem that are to our advantage, and others that most definitely are not. First the good news: the Catholics really aren't that good at Bible studies.

Most of them don't know the first thing about the Bible. They don't know Zacchaeus from Ezekiel and are likely to think that the Epistle to the Philippians was written to Catholics in the Philippines. Their ignorance is astounding. In addition, (with a few exceptions) they don't have the concept that the Scriptures are powerful or personal in any way.

They view the Bible as a dull tome from which they hear readings at Mass that they do not understand. The idea that the enemy might speak to them personally through the Scriptures is simply not in their toolbox.

I'm also happy to say that those Catholics who do study the Scriptures have been influenced by the progress we have made with the Protestants. We've managed to infiltrate Catholic seminaries and Biblical institutes with the same 'higher criticism'. With any luck the person leading your patient's Bible study will be thoroughly versed in the 'higher critical approach' and he may just turn the whole thing into an academic exercise studying the reliability of the text. I had one patient—a Catholic layman— who spent months with a parish Bible study group trying to decide whether the Sermon on the Mount was really a sermon and whether it really was delivered on a mountain or not.

The bad news is we have not found it quite so easy to get Catholics to make the Bible say whatever they want it to say. The downside of them not being aware of a personal meaning for the Scriptures is that they often believe in the Church's interpretation instead.

Catholics really do believe that their church interprets the Bible. As a result they are likely to read the Scriptures with that prissy little tome of theirs called the Catechism. Some of them have a whole library of their church's writings on the Scriptures right back over the last miserable two thousand years. There are one or two out there who used to be Protestants. They have come into the Catholic Church with a vast knowledge of the Bible and they have added to it a deep understanding of the Church's historic teachings.

Furthermore, they communicate like professionals. They write books, they record tapes, they go on speaking tours. They are doing an immense amount of damage Bracket. These are the ones you want to trample. If you come across a Catholic who is able to place the Scriptures within the whole teaching of the Catholic Church, and he teaches with enthusiasm and passion; wreck him. Find his weakness and wreck him.

I fear that young priest may be one of them. Glimtongue tells me he used to be a Baptist. Not good Bracket. If your patient falls under his spell you will have your work cut out for you. Be prepared to accompany your patient as he starts reading the dullest books imaginable. You may have to be at his elbow as he reads Bible commentaries, books of apologetics and paperback editions of the Apostolic Fathers.

If so, consider it your punishment for the slip ups over the weekend.

Slubgrip

WEEK SIX ~ *Thursday*

My dear Knobby,

You can imagine the hurt I felt when I discovered that our old friend Grimkin had passed the complaints of those two scoundrels Snozzle and Crasston on to you.

I'm sorry you have to be troubled with such petty concerns and squabbles amongst us lesser beings. Really Knobby, I must ask you to trust me on this one. Snozzle and Crasston are expert at appearing plausible while all the time they are undermining, blackmailing and smearing others. I'm not the first of their victims, and I expect I won't be the last. If you give them any credence at all, you may find yourself their next victim. They're ambitious Knobby, and their ambition is limitless.

I'm more than happy to come and explain the charges against me. Once you hear the whole story I'm sure you will understand and my name will be cleared.

Your suggested time and place for a meeting suits me perfectly. I'll come under my own steam. You needn't send the Flancks and the Black Widow.

I'll see you on Saturday,

Yrs,

Slubgrip

Corpulous,

Did you get Crasston and Snozzle to change their story? I realize it's not pleasant when you have to apply some pressure with Cerebus, but I hope it worked.

I really do need to hear from you quite soon one way or the other. Write to me Corpulous. I need information

Slubgrip

Britwiggle,

Were you able to plant that story about Snozzle and Crasston with your friend in Knobby's secretariat? It's important that I hear from you dear girl. Things are getting a bit sticky here, and I need to know if you are on my side.

Drop me a line as soon as possible,

Slubgrip

WEEK SIX ~ *Friday*

Bracket,

Things are not good. You know Friday is my bad day, and my headaches are particularly bad today. In addition to my sinuses I've had news that the charges Crasston and Snozzle have fabricated against me have made it all the way to Knobswart. To make matters worse, both Grimkin and Knobby seem to believe Crasston and Snozzle.

I hope I can count on you Bracket, to take my side. You know from the beginning of our short relationship I have supported and helped you in every way. I consider it an honor to have you as my colleague, and hope I can depend on you to help me stamp out the ridiculous stories that Snozzle and Crasston are spreading about me.

So you can support me adequately I should perhaps tell you about my 'little problem' in the past. A few centuries ago, when I was a much younger tempter, I experienced a few setbacks. These things happen in the rough and tumble of our exalted life, and it is my opinion that they should be written off as a learning opportunity. What happened was this: I was looking after a young Spanish fellow who was a soldier. I had been very successful with him, and he was making nice progress towards a military career, an outwardly respectable life and enough wealth and power to make him forget the enemy completely. I managed to get him wounded in the wars, and perhaps that was my first blunder. I couldn't resist the pleasure in seeing him being hit by that cannonball.

Well, I thought when he was in recovery I had him. He was feeling sorry for himself and I even nudged him very nicely from self pity to despair. He was in pain and it was only one more little step to get him to end his own life.

Then I shifted my attention for just a moment and the enemy's agent was there. I had underestimated him. He got my patient to read some old books on chivalry and then got him to read the Scriptures. The next thing I knew he had shifted sides completely and was (to use the enemy's term) thoroughly converted. He went on to found that despicable pretend army called the Jesuits.

Believe me Bracket, the memories down below are very long. Somehow Crasston and Snozzle discovered this in the archives and they have been using it against me. When Dogwart failed so miserably things got worse for me. Why they should hold me responsible for the fat slug's failings I have no idea, but that's how it works. You can see that my own fate depends largely on your success with your patient. I've had a new report about him from Glimtongue, and apparently he is even more serious about his Catholic faith than we first thought.

Did you know Bracket that he has actually had a conversation with that nauseating priest about becoming a priest himself? The situation is desperate Bracket, and I suggest we both get off our haunches and get to battle stations.

Yrs,

Slubgrip

WEEK SIX ~ *Saturday*

His Excellency Undersecretary Knobswart
Lower Secretariat of Enquiries
Ninth circle

Excellency,

I understand that Slubgrip is due to see you today, and that, in recognition of his seniority; you have not sent the Flancks and the Black Widow. I think this is wise, but I would advise you not to be taken in by Slubgrip. I have evidence that he has asked Britwiggle to plant negative stories about Crasston and Snozzle within your secretariat, and that he has sent Corpulous with Cerebus to 'encourage' Crasston and Snozzle to change their story. After centuries of Slubgrip's political maneuverings, I think you and I are very aware of his procedural methods.

I advise you to double check any negative stories about Crasston and Snozzle with your own intelligence. If they should suddenly change their story in favor of Slubgrip, dismiss their witness. It is the result of torture. You know how three bites from Cerebus makes any of these cowards change their mind. Should these things occur today Knobswart, know that I speak the truth.

In fact I have been following Slubgrip's descent into incompetence every step of the way. Dogwart was the first to bring it to my attention, and now Bracket and Snoot have provided very effective inside information. Knobby, although Slubgrip would like us to forget it, is it really possible not to remember the absolute pig's ear he made of that young man in Spain in the sixteenth century? Countless souls were won for the enemy's cause and our own everlasting agenda was set back by hundreds of years. Practically the whole of the South American continent was lost because of Slubgrip, and has he ever received the punishment that was due? I think not. Instead he has charmed, schemed and deceived his way back into a very influential position, and I should remind you Knobswart, that he has taken every chance to undermine your authority, bad mouth you to others (in his urbane way of course) and to set himself up for election to your post once he got you ousted.

The time has come to put Slubgrip in his place. He constantly plays the 'old friend' card with both of us, and I for one, am heartily sick and tired of it. He's a boring old cad, and have you noticed how badly he smells? Sulfur and decay hangs around him like a miasmal mist. He's stopped looking after himself Knobswart. He's a disgrace to the College of Tempters. His horns are scabby, his fur is infested, he has mange, his wings are tattered and his fangs are broken and yellow.

Now I come to my real point. All of the other things wouldn't matter except that he has simply failed in his duties. Dogwart's failure with this dangerous young Catholic is really Slubgrip's fault. A lazy tempter like Dogwart needed strong handling, a nip at the heels and the odd prod with a pitchfork—right where it hurts. Slubgrip observed Dogwart's demise with a careless attitude. He didn't really do much at all to help Dogwart succeed apart from the odd scolding now and then. When Dogwart fell, Slubgrip was the first to gobble him up. Dogwart should have been yours Knobswart—that's how the pyramid tempting system works, but no, Slubgrip grabbed him.

Now that Bracket is on the case things are not much better. We all had high hopes for Bracket, but when we knew that Slubgrip would still be the mentor we knew it wouldn't be long before another major disaster was on our hands. Now Bracket is throwing up his hands in frustration. Slubgrip is no help at all. He sends long letters about theology, lecturing poor Bracket in his pompous way on things he already knows, and instead of rallying the troops to help Bracket with a very difficult young patient, Slubgrip spends his time scheming and plotting to remove first myself, and then you.

Furthermore, have you heard about his disastrous handling of his own patient? Slubgrip hasn't let this out, but I know from some other tempters who were there that Slubgrip's version of the events when his patient went to the healing Mass are completely untrue. Slubgrip said the man and his wife left the service in disgust as soon as the healing started. In fact the opposite happened. The man's wife convinced him to stay, and eventually he went forward and received the laying on of hands from that nun with the so called 'healing gift'.

The man fell over in a swoon and lay on the floor for a full twenty minutes. When he got up he was weeping and claiming to be healed. The enemy must have pulled one of his tricks, because the man went to his doctor the next day and all the signs of his cancer had disappeared.

To make matters worse, Slubgrip's patient has had a complete change of heart regarding his former concerns. He still loves the traditional old Mass, but now he does so with a new fervor and simplicity that is truly alarming.

The time for action has come Excellency. I hope you will move immediately. You know you have my totally loyal support.

Yrs Sincerely,

Grimkin

PASSION WEEK ~ *Palm Sunday*

My Dear Bracket,

Thank you so much for expressing concern about my meeting with Knobby yesterday. It all went swimmingly. He apologized for dragging me all the way down there and we had a very nice little luncheon together. A light fricassee of gossips followed by a sweet roll of hoarders. Knobby keeps some of the best staff for himself, and dining at Enquiries House is always a treat.

After reminiscing about old times Knobby told me not to worry about Crasston and Snozzle at all. It seems some rather nasty stories about them have turned up in the secretariat and Knobby said he had no intention of believing silly rumors from the clerks and janitors instead of myself. Then, wouldn't you know it Bracket, but in the middle of luncheon Crasston and Snozzle themselves showed up! I must say they were looking the worse for wear. It looked like they had been up all night wrestling with a three headed dog or something. It was the surprise of my life! To top it all both of the rascals fell on their knees before old Knobby and confessed that they had been lying about me and that they were scheming not only to take my place, but to supplant Knobby himself!

Well, the place was in an uproar! Knobby rose from the table in an volcanic rage. I don't know if you have ever seen one of his rages Bracket. He's usually a perfect lamb, as you know, but the wolf is always just beneath the surface, and when he snarls it is truly impressive. Poor Snozzle and Crasston were all quivering jelly and looked positively delighted when the Flancks came in and marched them off to be carted away in the Black Widow.

I've been vindicated Bracket, and to show his regard for me, Knobswart has asked me to join him at the Secretariat. Apparently there is a vacancy in the catering department. I admit, it is not the position I would have wanted for myself, but it is a promotion just to be asked to work at the Secretariat, and eventually one maybe able to work one's way up. Everyone admits that I have a penchant for this sort of thing, and I expect in a few decades I'll be Knobby's right hand man. In the meantime, Knobby's asked me to oversee the menus for ceremonial dinners. Apparently my mixture of humor, fine bile and delicious cooking at Dogwart's 'awards dinner' has made me somewhat of a *cause celebre* and Knobby wants me to organize similar events.

This means Bracket, that our short lived relationship is over. I've been instructed by the lowerarchy to move on immediately and hand my patient over to Grimkin. You will be answering to Hardcastle, one of the shock troops being drafted in to help you look after your young Catholic patient. Word is out that the situation there is becoming very dangerous and an expert is being called in who knows how to handle enthusiastic young Catholics. She's been working very successfully for many years in most of the major Catholic universities and high schools across the world with wonderful results for our side.

So I bid you a fond farewell Bracket. I have learned much from you dear boy. I'll keep an eye on you, and if you ever want a decent meal at the Secretariat, just look me up.

All best,

Slubgrip

PASSION WEEK ~ *Monday*

Bracket,

I'm in charge now, and I have no time for the polite talk and charming style of that decadent snob Slubgrip. Desperate times call for desperate measures. This is an important week for your patient Bracket. There will be no rest. Start today and start the attack. Remember the motto: Eat or be eaten.

Here's what you are going to do. First of all, do everything to make sure that your patient has some kind of physical accident. I want a physical injury Bracket, and none of your suave head games please. I know his enemy agent is vigilant and will guard him against harm if he can. That's just one of the challenges you have to face. Get on with it. I want a seriously painful injury by tomorrow or I'll have your guts for garters.

Second: throw him in a tailspin over this new girl. She's going to write him a nasty letter. I want a good old fashioned fight over it. Loosen him up with a drink or two first if you need to, then I want a confrontation. Snoot will make sure she is on her prissy high horse and I want your boy foaming at the mouth with pain from his injury, rage, frustration and sexual tension. Get him to hit her if you can. I want to see some real passion in this Bracket.

Third: make sure the upset affects his faith. He was traipsing along thinking this girl was a cross between Maria in *The Sound of Music* and the 'Little Flower of Lisieux'. Show him that his Miss Catholic Universe is a spoiled, sexually repressed brat, and make that undermine his faith big time. I want him not only to walk out on her. I want him to walk out on his faith.

Fourth: this is the foul week they call 'Holy Week'. Your patient is going to forget all about his new found love for the church, the miserable little priest friend of his, and the rest of that religious clap trap. He's going to get totally caught up in the little soap opera we're preparing for him, and his head will be spinning so fast he won't know whether it's Holy Week or Hell Week.

Get to work you stuck up ponce, or the Flancks will be at your door.

Hardcastle

Snoot,

I'm taking over from that fat good for nothing snob, Slubgrip. Here are your marching orders: I want your prissy little patient to have a big time bust up with Bracket's boy. I don't care how you make it happen, but she's going to write him a snooty little letter cutting off their relationship that makes his blood boil.

I want that done by tomorrow you little vixen or you'll find yourself pursued by the hounds of hell. Got it?

As soon as possible there will be a confrontation. He'll respond and I want her as uptight and prissy as a frustrated nun. She will insult him and put him down. He will hit her. I want blood to run Snoot, and if there's no blood it's your fault.

Get on with it or you'll find yourself in the Black Widow on the way to the Bog.

Hardcastle

PASSION WEEK ~ *Tuesday*

To His Lowliness, Undersecretary Knobswart

Excellency,

Now that I have taken over Slubgrip's patient, I have to report that things are far worse than we first thought. His patient did, indeed go forward at the healing Mass to receive prayer from the nun. It is not true that he was healed however. The medical condition is actually much more serious than anyone thought, the patient's cancer is advancing rapidly and he may have only a few weeks left to live. This news would be welcome, but what did happen at the healing Mass is even worse than a physical healing.

Somehow all the fear and rage about his condition that he should be experiencing has disappeared. He has received the news that he has a very short time to live with an unfortunate equanimity that I seem to have no power over. This is the worst possible situation: the patient has time to focus on his impending death, put his house in order and prepare to die. A sudden accident or a long drawn out illness, by which we can bankrupt him and bring him to despair, is far better. As it stands, the man has the support of his wife and friends, and he has decided to enter the local hospice for the dying which is run by that abominable order of sisters.

Slubgrip should have seen this coming and arranged for an accident while the man was still in a state of hatred and self righteousness. Now the illness has had the opposite effect. The man is quiet, submissive to the enemy's will and is actually joking about 'the other side' and wondering whether he'll meet his loved ones who have already died. It is most unpleasant, Knobswart. I've now got to try somehow to rescue the fellow, and clean up the mess Slubgrip left behind.

I'll have to resort to the emergency tactics in the textbook and rely on my own experience. Happily the priests are all busy this week, and we can delay any 'last rites' the superstitious fools might want to perform. With any luck I will be able to get the patient back into a state of denial, then switch him suddenly back to his real condition. He wants to face death does he? I'll work with archives in the meantime and bring all his past sins back to him. He'll see what a selfish, lustful and proud person he's been and I may be able to nudge him first into fear, and then into despair and make him forget to call the priest.

It will mean non-stop work Knobswart, but I'll do this, and should be able to succeed, knowing that some real skill shown at this late stage will eventually reflect back on you and on our whole division.

About Slubgrip: I was pleased to hear about his promotion to your catering department. It was a stroke of genius Knobswart, and I look forward to Slubgrip's 'ceremonial dinner' on Thursday night.

Your loyal servant, Grimkin

PASSION WEEK ~ *Wednesday*

Bracket,

You did well. I must admit, when I saw your filed horns and the filigree work on your wings, I doubted whether you had the potential for the rough stuff that is required sometimes.

You patient falling off the chair when he was changing a light bulb was just the right amount of violence. His bad back kept him irritable and frustrated. Working with his parents' tempters to get them out of the house for a few days was a fine touch. That's the sort of team work that's required for success. Getting them out of the house meant you could increase his loneliness, and going without his mothers' good cooking would make him tetchy and cross.

The email from Snoot's girl was perfectly written. I loved her phrase "I have prayed about this, and I really believe God does not want me to see you anymore because you will be a bad influence." It set his insecurity and pride alight at the same time, and got him ready for the punch up. Bracket, how did you get the pipsqueak to have the courage to actually go around to her house? I expect you played on his sense of drama and self importance. Did you paint a picture in his mind of Romeo beneath the balcony? Did he go around to declare his love?

You and Snoot handled it perfectly! She had her girl already in her nightgown pretending to pray when he turned up outside her window. Snoot tells me that she made sure the girl mistook the scene completely and thought your boy was sneaking a peek at her while changing, and that she went completely over the top, nearly calling the police.

I have to hand it to both of you. The final scene was a brilliant piece of stage management. Him trying to explain himself, her crying with fear and frustration! It was priceless. Good going.

I know I asked you for some blood, but if he didn't actually hit her, it's alright. The fact that he called her a "stuck up little bitch" was pretty good. I think that will be enough to end that dangerous dalliance for good, and I applaud the skill and subtlety with which you and Snoot handled it.

Don't let this little victory go to your head Bracket. You may have won the battle. You have not won the war until the little rodent comes to his proper home below. Remember, the enemy can turn the tables on you in a flash, and the great triumph you thought you attained will be snatched from you.

Keep at it. This is an especially dangerous week. I want you to use the break up as a way to keep gnawing at him. Keep his resentment and hurt on the boil. Keep his anger and frustration cooking away. Keep running the scene in his mind and make him imagine "what he should have said." Build the anger, rage and resentment until it becomes an obsession. Make sure he always blames her and never sees his own weaknesses.

This is full time work Bracket. Don't imagine that you'll have time off. Now I'm in charge I hope you'll realize that this is not a game.

Hardcastle.

Maundy Thursday

To: His Honor Grimkin STD
Office of the Diabolical Council of Enquiries
Eighth Circle

Dear Grimkin

I'm sorry you were not able to make it to Slubgrip's 'ceremonial dinner' earlier this evening, but I understand that you could not leave your patient's side, and I applaud your diligence.

Slubrip was buttered up (as it were) beforehand with everyone telling him how his Dogwart Dinner was such an amusing surprise. I took him into my confidence and told him that Snozzle and Crasston were going to be brought to the dinner and that he should prepare a similar 'surprise' for them. Slubgrip worked for hours putting the menu together, and preparing how he would surprise Crasston and Snozzle. Of course, Crasston and Snozzle and the rest of my staff, were in on the hoax. All the time Slubgrip was gloating and laughing about the fate of Snozzle and Crasston and the kitchen staff were pretending to enjoy the joke. The menu was prepared and Slubgrip called the main course 'Dialobical Surprise'

I asked Slubgrip to present each course with a special procession of honor. The greed soup was served in bowls that looked like little purses, and brought in by waiters dressed as stockbrokers. Slubgrip's second course was a fine fillet of slothful youth. This was served with scalp chips by some of the fat, pimply slugs from the eighth circle. The lust lava was brought in by some of Britwiggle's team trussed up in the most outrageous lingerie. I must admit, poor old Slubgrip does have a gift for drama and a certain refinement of humor.

Then Slubgrip stepped forward to give a speech about his 'Diabolical Surprise." He went on at some length about Dogwart and his stupidity and how he had to pay for his crimes. Then I had him finish with the phrase, "And tonight's Diabolical Surprise is..."

He thought the crowd was primed to scream out "Crasston and Snozzle" Instead they howled and roared out 'Slubgrip, Slubgrip, Slubgrip!"

At first Slubgrip thought they were howling out their praise for him, and he smiled and gave one of his ridiculous gentlemanly bows.

At last it dawned on him that he had prepared his own diabolical surprise. My dear Grimkin, talk about "Last Suppers", it was certainly a night to remember. Once he realized what had happened, Slubgrip panicked. He looked around for a supporter of some kind and realized that everyone had abandoned him. Snozzle and Crasston were already at the rotisserie stoking up the flames, and when the Flancks came and grabbed him, Slubgrip went down with all the self importance and pomposity and all the outraged protestations you would expect. It was one of the most amusing nights I've had for centuries.

The after dinner speeches were the usual raucous ones mocking the victim's faults and gloating over his eventual demise. Sowerage explained how Slubgrip would re-emerge in the sewers of the lowest realms, and that since he is an eternal being, his digested parts would re-congeal and he would be starting out from the very lowest realm of existence with the paramecium, worms and maggots.

I finished the evening with a few words of warning for anyone else who might think they can supplant me or overthrow the lowerarchy of our division.

Grimkin, I am aware that tonight is one of horror for us, and I planned Slubgrip's surprise as a consolation for the troops as the enemy agents move into this most horrible and revolting three days of the year.

It is a horrid time Grimkin. Each year I think it will not be so bad, that the enemy's little sleight of hand two thousand years ago will not enrage me as much as it has in the past, but every time it starts up again my bile boils. When I think of that pompous rabbi calling himself the Son of God and piously telling his disciples that they must 'eat his flesh and drink his blood' I seethe with rage. Imagine him stealing all our best imagery! For millennia we had the pagan priests doing human sacrifices quite nicely on our behalf. For ages we had the humans consuming one another in ceremonial cannibalism, and with one little get together with his pathetic tribe he snatches it all away from us, and puts his own puerile ceremony in its place.

Our priests and priestesses did really useful things. They cast spells, told fortunes, put curses on people, worked as temple prostitutes, plucked hearts out of their victims, beheaded children and eviscerated virgins for fun. He comes along and creates priests who are insufferable goody goodies, doing nothing but some inane bit of hocus pocus with a cookie and grape juice and going around being nice, feeding the poor and 'forgiving' everyone, and tonight all over the world they'll gather and make a big deal out of it.

I'm feeling quite depressed about the whole thing. I'm going back to the banquet hall. There's half a haunch of Slubgrip left. It will be nice with a slop of that grouch gravy, and a slurp of red bile.

Gloomily yrs,

Knobswart

Good Friday

Knobby,

It was good of you to write and tell me about Slubgrip's "Last Supper". I'll relish the memory for years. It was very thoughtful of you to send Crasston and Snozzle with that portion of Slubgrip's underbelly. It fried up quite nicely for my breakfast.

You asked for an update of Slubgrip's man. Things are going as well as can be expected. The progress of the cancer is very fast now, and it looks like the old boy is giving up. Of course, the horrid hospice nurses are doing everything they can to alleviate his pain, so it's pretty difficult to use that one to bring him down. His two sons and daughter have turned up to "say good bye." He was estranged from one son, hated his son in law and the other son stayed in the old man's good books to get on the good side of the will. I pointed all this out to him while he was lying on the deathbed, but he seemed willing to let all that slide, and I'm sorry to report that there were the usual deathbed scenes of forgiveness, tears and goodwill.

There is one good thing: he's also not talking to his wife. I reminded him of the time she was unfaithful twenty years ago, and I've got him nursing that grudge quite nicely.

What enrages me is that these are all things that Slubgrip should have been working on, but he was a lazy maggot, and it is a relief to know that he will soon be a maggot once more.

Despite Slugrip's negligence, I think I can say that the patient will still be ours. Unfortunately, as you know, this is not something I can guarantee. The enemy agents have are always ready to cheat and snatch the souls that should be ours from under our nose with one of their annoying little reversals, and until we have better intelligence, it is impossible for us to judge which way the souls of the hairless bipeds will go.

I'm sorry this update is so short Knobswart, but you know how our entire army comes down with migraine headaches on this day. The enemy never lets us forget our Father's unfortunate blunder on that Friday two thousand years ago.

The enemy was devious. Without complete intelligence, how was our father below to know that the rag tag rabbi was anything more than another one of the enemy's prophets? That he really was the enemy in human form was something no self respecting devil could have imagined possible. How could he, who is above all, have lowered himself to become one of the snot dribbling, snoring, defecating hairless chimpanzees? It was a sneaky, low down trick.

I'm furious just thinking about our Father's unfortunate humiliation. No wonder on this day our entire army comes down with a migraine. It's three o'clock, and mine is terrible. I feel claustrophobic. I have to get out. My head feels like it is in a vise that is slowly closing.

I am in agony Knobswart. My head is splitting, and I'm furious. It's insufferable. It never should have happened. Someone will pay for this. You wait and see if I don't get my own back....

Despairingly,

Grimkin

Holy Saturday

Bracket,

If the reports I hear are true you and Snoot will both make a dainty dish to set before the King. Glimtongue tells me your young Catholic patient not only went to the Good Friday liturgy yesterday, but he went to confession, and is planning to attend the Easter Vigil tonight. What are you doing about it slacker? You may have had a small triumph the other day, but don't you realize that is exactly the time to double your efforts? It's after one of our victories that the little worms are most likely to go running off to the enemy.

Furthermore, these three days every year the enemy and his agents are out in force. This oily light he calls 'grace' is flooding everywhere. Why he insists on pouring this gift of himself into the little vermin is beyond me. He has no sense of dignity Bracket. It's like giving gold pieces to paupers—they only waste it on themselves. Yet still he pours out his 'grace' everywhere, and these three days you will find that whenever you try to do anything you've got to wade through the gooey light. It's like wading through chest deep oily acid. I don't know about you, but yesterday's annual migraine was one of the worst. I was laid low completely and could barely move.

But it's back to the front today. I've asked Britwiggle to get on the inside of Snoot's girl's family, and she says the girl is tormenting herself over her argument with your boy, and it has only made her realize how much she really cares for the pimply pipsqueak. You had better get your act together, and do something quickly or all will be lost.

I'll have Snoot get her girl to invite the boy to talk. With any luck they will both skip the Easter vigil. Getting them to make up would be better than both of them going off to the church together. After these horrid three days are over we can get back to work on splitting them up. You just make sure the boy concentrates on her and doesn't see the young priest in action. I sense something serious going on between those two, and from what you've said, the enemy agents have put up some screens.

Stay on it Bracket.

Hardcastle

Snoot,

Get off your sweet little tail my girl, there's work to be done. Get your girl to invite Bracket's boy out to kiss and make up, and make sure they stay out too late to go to the Easter vigil.

Something is happening between the boy and the young priest, and the enemy agents have put up some of their light screens so we can't see what's going on.

It's up to you Snoot. Remember...Eat or be eaten.

Hardcastle

.

EASTER SUNDAY

Grimkin,

Blaming Slubgrip for your failure will get you nowhere. You are an experienced enough tempter never to have let this happen. I understand that you took on your patient at the last moment, but there is no excuse for your allowing the priest to administer the last rites. Why didn't you network with the priest's tempter and remind the priest how busy he was and suggest that he could go to see the patient within a few days?

You should have known that during these three days the enemy is especially busy. He is busy pouring out his 'forgiveness' and 'grace' with embarrassing abundance. The sentimentality of it all is quite appalling. I once had a perfectly cynical patient who was close to death at Christmas. He was locked into despair and about to breathe his last when a group of young people from the local Catholic High School came to the nursing home to sing Christmas carols. A young girl sang 'Away in the Manger' and my patient melted into a mess of sickly religious sentiment. The enemy agent jumped in, and after the priest gave the blessing and was about to go out the door my patient called him over and asked to make his confession.

I know how unfair you feel it all is. You have slaved away at a dull and thankless task for years, and the enemy steps in at the last minute and snatches away your reward. The fact that they do so with their insufferable lightness of touch and insouciance is maddening. The enemy's agents seem to accomplish their victories with so little effort. They waltz along singing their inane songs of praise and laughing amongst themselves in that superior way of theirs, and then, "Oh look, the Master has saved another soul. Let us rejoice shall we?" It makes me sick.

Then as you're grinding your teeth and trying to retain your dignity in the face of defeat, they pretend you're not there and open their unbearable doors of light to the patient. I know how it burns. I know how you shrink and shrivel in the light like a slug that's been salted. Perhaps I should feel sorry for you Grimkin, but I don't. You know the rules of the game, and you know what happens when you lose.

The fact of the matter is, you have lost a soul Grimkin, and your punishment is the usual one. All promotions are cancelled and you will be assigned a new soul that is born tomorrow. It's back to square one for you. You'll have to endure all the first stages of a patient in infancy. I hope you enjoy the boredom of playtime, the smelly diapers and the endless atmosphere of affection, sweetness and light that surrounds their babies.

Enjoy yourself, and don't try taking any shortcuts by killing the brat, or we'll see you at dinner.

Knobswart

From: His Excellency Knobswart
Undersecretariat of Enquiries

Bracket,

Hardcastle and Britwiggle have reported the most appalling news. It is true that she instructed you and Snoot to get your patients together, but how could you and Snoot have allowed such an occurrence to take place?

Hardcastle and Britwiggle tell me that the boy and girl met on Saturday night, and did indeed miss the vigil Mass, but that they stayed up late talking into the wee hours. Not only have they kissed and made up as commanded, but I'm told they have become best of friends.

Best of friends, Bracket, is worse than lovers. Best of spiritual friends is the worst possible outcome. Are the reports true that these 'best of friends' are now encouraging each other to discern their religious vocations? What have we got here? A budding Francis and Clare? A nascent Heloise and Abelard? A little Teresa of Calcutta and Karol Wojtyla? How could you and Snoot allow this to happen? I realize that these three days are especially hard going, and I expect the boy and girl's enemy agents were on a roll, blocking you out and outmaneuvering you on every turn.

I know your frustration. Just when you think you have got your patient figured out he goes and makes some totally unpredictable decision. It's because the enemy really has given them a portion of his power called free will. Because of this, when the battle is going on, it only takes a slight move on their part to align themselves with what the enemy wants them to do.

We're battling upstream all the time. The only hope we have is to blind our patients to the enemy's message, and get them into our own habits, and after a very long time of constant work we may get them to the point where they no longer make these unpredictable decisions that turn our plans upside down. Even then, after a lifetime in our service some of the vermin still turn tail and run for the enemy just when you weren't expecting.

So I understand how sudden the reversal can be, but that is no excuse. The long and the short of it is, you are now dealing with a young man who is very enthusiastic about the fact that he has 'found his vocation' to the priesthood, and he is feeling all sentimental about the young woman in a totally unerotic way. Furthermore he is feeling all 'spiritual' because his calling happened during Lent. Snoot has got to deal with a young woman who really thinks she could be a religious sister, and can't wait to visit the convent for one of their 'days of discernment.' Worst of all, Hardcastle tells me that both the girl and the boy talked about spiritual warfare, and that they seemed aware that the bust up earlier in the week had 'something weird' or 'something supernatural' about it. This means your cover is blown and you and Snoot will be transferred.

With immediate effect Hardcastle is taking over Snoot's girl, and I'm sending Pertwee to take charge of your boy. Snoot is being given a third grade girl complete with a set of Barbie dolls, and your new charge is a fourteen year old boy who does nothing but play computer games all day. These patients are more your speed I think....

At this point the communications were interrupted and engineers were unable to re-establish the computer feed.

Two days later another fragment was recovered and de-coded...

Another year has begun tempters. Battle stations all. We have discovered that there has been a leak in our communications systems and some of the correspondence between members of Excellency Knobswart's division have been intercepted and de-coded by the enemy's subjects. This is an unforgivable offence.

New codes have now been established and the necessary re-shuffle has occurred. Knobswart has been removed to circle eleven in order to be suitably re-educated. With immediate effect Crasston assumes responsibility for the Undersecretariat of Enquiries with Snozzle as his deputy....

Transmission lost...

MORE BOOKS ~ *By Dwight Longenecker*

If you enjoyed *The Gargoyle Code* why not check out Fr. Longenecker's other books? You can order any of them through his website:

www.dwightlongenecker.com

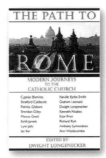

The Path to Rome - Fr. Longenecker used to be an Anglican priest. After he converted to the Catholic faith in 1995 he edited this collection of conversion stories.

Sixteen people tell how and why they became Catholics. From a former Anglican Bishop of London, to a woman Salvation Army Officer, from EWTN host Marcus Grodi to an Anglican priest's wife they all tell their moving and inspiring stories of why they took The Path to Rome

More Christianity - Evangelical Christians love the Lord Jesus Christ and follow him with honest and open hearts. However, there is more to the Christian faith. Catholics affirm all the good things Evangelicals affirm, they just don't deny some of the things Evangelicals deny.

Fr. Longenecker was brought up as an Evangelical and attended Bob Jones University. He understands Evangelicals and in this book he explains the Catholic faith to Evangelicals with good humor, grace, simplicity and clarity. He's not concerned to prove Evangelicals wrong. Instead he urges them to move from 'Mere Christianity' to something more.

Mary-A Catholic Evangelical Debate - Twenty years after graduating from Bob Jones University Dwight Longenecker met up with an old college buddy through the internet. By this time Dwight was a Catholic and David Gustafson was an Evangelical attending an Episcopal Church. After many months debating religion by email, Dwight and David decided to put their minds to writing a book on the Blessed Virgin Mary.

David takes the Protestant side of the debate and Dwight explains and defends all the Catholic beliefs and practices regarding the Virgin Mary. With introductions from Protestant scholar J.I.Packer and Catholic Fr. Richard John Neuhaus, this book is a readable but well researched study of everything you always wanted to know about Mary.

St. Benedict and St. Therese-The Little Rule and the Little Way - During his time living in England, Fr. Longenecker developed a great interest in both St. Benedict and St. Therese of Lisieux. This book studies the lives and writings of these two beloved saints.

St. Benedict is like the grandfather in the family of God and Therese is like his little grandchild. Together they complement one another and show us how to find God in the ordinary things of life.

Listen My Son - St. Benedict for Fathers - As a father of four children and a Benedictine oblate, Fr. Dwight Longenecker is ideally suited to apply the famous *Rule of St. Benedict* to family life.

This book of daily readings give the reader a portion from the *Rule of St. Benedict* for each day. After the portion from the Rule there is a short reading that applies the timeless wisdom of St. Benedict to modern family life. This is a great gift for fathers of all ages.

Adventures in Orthodoxy - This unusual book take the reader on a Chestertonian rollercoaster ride through the Apostle's Creed. Fr Longenecker goes on a creative quest for truth showing that orthodox Christianity is anything but dull. Instead it is a wide open, exciting explanation for all that was, all that is, and all that shall be.

Noted biographer Joseph Pearce has said, "In this exciting book Longenecker follows in the imaginative footsteps of Chesterton and Lewis. He sees and seizes the thrill of truth with insights of pyrotechnic brilliance. He shows us that orthodoxy is dynamic and thrilling. Hold on tight and enjoy the ride!"

Praying the Rosary for Inner Healing - God has used this book to touch thousands of lives. In a very practical and simple way, Fr Longenecker shows how the twenty mysteries of the rosary connect with the different stages of our lives. Step by step, this book helps the reader meditate on the stages of Christ's life and open their deepest areas of their lives to the healing graces of Christ.

With inspiring illustrations by Catholic artist Chris Pelicano, *Praying the Rosary for Inner Healing* has been featured on the Spirit Daily website and on Johnette Benkovic's *Living His Life Abundantly*. It gives new direction for those already used to praying the rosary and shows newcomers how to use this ancient and beautiful form of prayer in a relevant and life changing way.

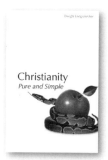

Christianity Pure & Simple - As the title says, this book explains the Christian faith in a simple, clear and direct manner. Steering clear of theological jargon, churchy language, liturgical code words and pious talk, *Christianity Pure & Simple* starts with arguments for the existence of God and moves through to the revelation of God in Jesus Christ, the coming of the Holy Spirit, the founding of the Church and the need for prayer and sacraments.

An excellent book for young people searching for the truth, this book has been used by home schoolers, high school and college students as a tool for evangelization a text book and a good first step for those who long for the fullness of God's truth.

A Sudden Certainty - Priest Poems This is a collection of Fr. Longenecker's poems. Written in traditional forms, but with a contemporary voice, Fr. Longenecker meditates on spiritual images alive in the ordinary life of a priest.

Each poem is a little window into a new way of seeing reality. Each page shows the reader a fresh way of connecting with God's light and love alive in the ordinary world.

In addition to his books, Fr. Longenecker writes regularly for *The National Catholic Register, This Rock Magazine, St Austin Review, Inside Catholic* and other websites. His popular and award winning blog, *Standing on My Head* is based on G.K.Chesterton's idea that, "Any scene can be more freshly and clearly seen when it is seen upside down."

Fr. Dwight has appeared on EWTN, Catholic radio and on broadcasts in England and across the USA. He speaks regularly and conferences and leads retreats on a variety of topics. Many audiences like to hear how he went from Bob Jones University to being a Catholic priest. Others ask him to lead retreats on the Benedictine and Theresian spirituality. He is also asked to lead workshops and seminars on apologetics, praying the rosary for inner healing, and his film-based seminars on *How to Be a Spiritual Hero.*

Fr. Longenecker is working on a new book called *How to Be a Spiritual Hero*, is trying to complete his conversion story and find the time to re-write his first novel, a screenplay on Shakespeare the Catholic, and his second book of verse.

Contact Fr. Longenecker through his website:
www.dwightlongenecker.com

BIOGRAPHY

Fr. Dwight Longenecker is an American who has spent most of his life living and working in England. After graduating from the fundamentalist Bob Jones University with a degree in Speech and English, he went to study theology at Oxford University. He was eventually ordained as an Anglican priest and served as a curate, a school chaplain in Cambridge and a country parson.

Realizing that he and the Anglican Church were on divergent paths, in 1995 Fr. Dwight and his family were received into the Catholic Church. He spent the next ten years working as a freelance Catholic writer, contributing to over twenty-five magazines, papers and journals in Britain, Ireland and the USA.

In 2006 Fr. Dwight accepted a post as Chaplain to St Joseph's Catholic School in Greenville, South Carolina. This brought him and his family back, not only to his hometown, but also to the American Bible belt, and hometown of Bob Jones University. In December of that year he was ordained as a Catholic priest under the special pastoral provision for married former Anglican clergy. In addition to his work at St Joseph's Catholic School he ministers in the parish of St Mary's, Greenville.

Fr. Dwight enjoys movies, blogging, books, and visiting Benedictine monasteries. He's married to Alison. They have four children, named Benedict, Madeleine, Theodore and Elias. They live in Greenville, South Carolina with assorted pets including a black Labrador named Anna.